Through his many years as a counterterrorism operator and instructor with the NSW Police Tactical Operations Unit, Australian Federal Police and US Department of Defense, Shane Horsburgh knows a man's world like few others—but during a deployment to Iraq in 2006, Shane gained a new perspective on life. He recognised that the pressures and expectations placed on today's men to play the 'macho game' did not allow for personal peace, prosperity and growth: vital elements in the pursuit of a more enjoyable life. Once back in Australia he concentrated on the inner workings of men and the motivations that drive them to live a life of dominance and conflict. An accomplished public speaker, Shane now delivers corporate, private and public sector programs confronting a number of issues inhibiting male growth, including the examination of what a 'real man' actually is. Shane also goes into schools to talk to teenage boys, where his positive message of self-understanding has had a profound impact on their lives.

Gift from Shane
Oct 2016

All The Best

FIGHTING BLIND

SHANE HORSBURGH

WITH JASON K. FOSTER

ALLEN&UNWIN
SYDNEY · MELBOURNE · AUCKLAND · LONDON

First published in 2012

Allen & Unwin
Sydney, Melbourne, Auckland, London

83 Alexander Street
Crows Nest NSW 2065
Australia

Phone: (61 2) 8425 0100
Fax: (61 2) 9906 2218
Email: info@allenandunwin.com
Web: www.allenandunwin.com

Cataloguing-in-Publication details are available
from the National Library of Australia
www.trove.nla.gov.au

ISBN 978 1 74237 879 4

Front cover images: author photograph, Wayne Bruce and David Gooley; helicopter,
iStockphoto.com/Rockfinder
Set in 12/17 pt Sabon by Post Pre-press, Sydney
Printed and bound in Australia by Griffin Press

10 9 8 7 6 5 4 3 2 1

Contents

1

Baghdad

'We are now beginning our descent into Baghdad International Airport. Please ensure your seatbelts are fastened and that your seats and tray tables are locked in the fully upright position.'

Over the years I've sat on hundreds of planes and whenever the flight attendants give the safety demonstration I usually look around the plane to see how many people are actually paying attention. Most of the time people are absorbed in their own worlds, listening to the radio or deciding which in-flight movie to watch. Generally, I'd be doing the same, but today I was hanging on the flight attendant's every word.

Fasten my seatbelt; you've got to be kidding, I thought as I looked down at the frayed mess of dilapidated threads stretching across my lap, noticing a distinct discolouration of the material I hadn't spotted earlier.

Great, I thought. *Someone has felt so scared they've had to vomit.*

Although dubious about its effectiveness, I clicked the buckle into place. My unease about this flight had begun two hours earlier when boarding the plane in Dubai. I strode confidently across the tarmac with my bag slung across my shoulder, but my bravado began to falter when I saw the ancient-looking Boeing 737 belonging to a budget subsidiary of Iraqi Air. I'd once read that the 737 was regarded as the 'work horse of the skies', owing to its popularity with various airlines across the world, but if this thing was a horse it should have been put out to pasture a long time ago.

Nevertheless, I'd accepted a job in Iraq and there was only one way I was going to get there. Reaching the top of the stairs, I entered the plane and was greeted by a stereotypical flight attendant: a good-looking, flawlessly manicured middle-aged woman wearing just a little too much make-up. It was a bit of a shame, really, because it diminished and disguised her natural beauty.

Amazing, I thought. *We're going into a war zone and people are still worried about how they look!*

I stood at the doorway waiting for her to ask to see my ticket and give me directions to my seat. No such luck. She just extended her arm towards the rather open single-class cabin. Fortunately, I was one of the first ones on the plane. I was left relatively alone and, after a little shoving, I managed to get a seat. Sitting there watching more and more people board reminded me of my youth, when we used to catch a banged-up old bus to school in the small country town where I grew up. Our daily ritual was to jostle, elbow and push for the best seat near somebody we knew, and as people continued to stream onto the plane I soon realised this was no different. It was like a game of musical chairs; people sitting on top of one another then looking around to find the nearest free seat, only to be beaten by a microsecond by someone else.

Absolute madness!

Happy to have a seat, I didn't really pay much attention to it or the state of my seatbelt but, after everything had calmed down and I actually took a good look, I was now seriously regretting my choice. The make-up-wearing flight attendant was still giving the safety demonstration and as I shifted around in my seat it began to move. I felt like an old man in a rocking chair. Looking around the cabin I soon realised my seat was the least of my worries. Roof panels hung from the ceiling, most of the carpets were ripped up and whole rows of seats were missing. In a last-ditch attempt to soothe my nerves I picked up one of the emergency evacuation cards from the magazine pocket on the seat in front and showed it to my companion, Matt. Quietly confident and unassuming, Matt was one of those blokes you liked from the first moment you met him. He was tall, athletically built and extremely fit, and we had become acquainted seven years earlier during a selection trial for counterterrorism operatives for the Sydney Olympics. We'd worked together ever since. It was great to catch up with him again in Dubai for the journey into Iraq but, more importantly, he'd done this trip a few times and I was very glad to be sitting next to him.

'Hey, mate. Have you ever noticed how calm people are in these pictures?' I said, almost shoving the card in his face.

'Not really, Horse!' Matt laughed.

Horse. I'd lived with that nickname since walking through the doors of the NSW Police Academy in 1989 as a brash young twenty-year-old recruit. My fellow classmates saw my surname, *Horsburgh*, emblazoned on my name tag and, in the Aussie tradition of shortening everybody's name, the moniker was born. Since then my real name had almost become redundant and I'd only ever hear it when speaking to my mum.

I wasn't complaining, though.

Sometimes people are labelled with nicknames they hate and end up being stuck with them for life. I remember one guy I worked with who earned the nickname 'Two Bums' on account of his rather ample backside. Understandably, he hated the name, but I didn't mind mine. It had proven to be more than useful as an icebreaker with women, who'd giggle as they looked me up and down.

Back in the plane I was still trying to get Matt to pay attention to the landing instructions.

'Look, mate, the plane is about to crash and they're smiling like Cheshire cats.'

'Don't be nervous, precious. Man up.'

'Fuck off! Who said I was nervous?'

'It's okay, mate. I was like that when I first flew in a year ago. Have you ever done any aerobatics flying?'

'Only when I accidentally put a glider into a spin when I was learning to fly as a teenager.'

'You're going to love this then.'

'Love what?'

'You'll see. I hope you didn't have too much breakfast.'

That explained my seatbelt's rainbow stain. I tried to change the subject to take my mind off any impending nausea.

'What are the other blokes like who we're going to work with?' I asked.

'Some really good blokes as well as some wankers— you'll fit right in!'

'Get fucked!'

Matt put on his own Cheshire smile.

I looked around the cabin. An eerie silence had descended over the other passengers. Some rocked back and forth, muttering the name of Allah over and over. *Great*, I thought. *They're praying to their god for protection. We must be in serious trouble!*

My worries were not eased by the fact the remaining passengers merely looked out the murky windows in quiet contemplation; as if they'd already resigned themselves to their fate. Suddenly, the calm and stable plane lurched to one side and dove into what can only be described as a surprising manoeuvre. The muttered prayers became loud incantations. Those who'd been in quiet contemplation also began to pray and, to be honest, I was beginning to find my religious side.

'Ah, is this normal?' I asked Matt as I was thrust violently back into my seat.

'Actually, mate, it is,' Matt said. 'It's been standard procedure ever since a civilian cargo plane got hit by a surface-to-air missile while taking off from Baggers a couple of years ago. Did you see anything like this in the Air Marshalls?'

'Not bloody likely! A week ago I was sitting in business class flying from LA to Sydney trying to decide whether to have the salmon or the chicken for lunch.'

'Ah, no sweat, mate, it'll be over soon. That's when the fun *really* begins.'

The plane, and my seat, began rocking more violently as I fought to keep my breakfast down. Flashbacks from my youth came thick and fast. I remembered the glider incident from when I was a sixteen-year-old trainee pilot. Flying just above a thousand feet, I attempted to turn the glider into a thermal air current but only succeeded in putting the aircraft into a potentially fatal spin, immediately drawing a panic-stricken stream of orders from the flight instructor in the rear seat. We somehow managed to land on the nearby airfield in one piece, albeit with a dirty set of underwear on my part.

Back in the cabin I tried to calm my mind. I just prayed the pilot knew what he was doing.

With my life seemingly hanging in the balance, I started to think about where I had been and where I was going. Grinning at the irony of it all, I found it hard to fathom how much had happened in a few short days. Less than a week ago I'd been working as a covert air security officer for the Australian Government, providing an armed, anti-hijacking capability on board Australian flag–carrying airlines as a consequence of the 9/11 attacks. I was the random guy sitting next to you. We might have smiled at each other or engaged in superficial conversation about the weather or our jobs, and you'd never have known the story I gave you was part of a carefully constructed narrative designed to conceal my true reason for flying. The best lies always have a healthy element of truth and my ruse was this: I was a risk-management consultant. After fifteen years in the police and nearly half of that in tactical operations and counterterrorism, I knew how to talk about managing risk. During the Sydney Olympics I conducted site surveys on most of the sporting venues to work out where and how our CT team would deploy in the event of a terrorist incident. Later, as a roping and rappelling instructor, I would look at training locations to assess their suitability and safety, even walking over the Sydney Harbour Bridge a few times to see if it would be suitable for us to abseil from. Not surprisingly, the bridge got the tick of approval and so did my cover story. I could easily draw on practical experience and theoretical knowledge to cement the deception, even while I was carrying a loaded Glock pistol under my shirt. I had been trained to use it if the need arose.

Luckily for me, I usually travelled in business class on domestic and international routes, so the ride was generally smooth, comfortable and safe—a stark contrast to where I now found myself.

Still in the throes of the downward spiral, the Iraqi plane's rickety airframe groaned heavily from the stresses placed on it by a hectic manoeuvre that I was sure didn't appear in any pilot training manual. Then, as suddenly as the plane had begun the manoeuvre, it now pulled out of the dive. Looking out the window I felt like I could almost touch the ground; our wings were barely level before the wheels were down and we were landing. We'd spiralled from twenty thousand feet to just over one thousand feet in a matter of minutes, a far cry from the long, slow, gentle approach to an airport to which I'd become accustomed.

'That's it, brother. Did you enjoy that?' Matt asked as the plane's wheels screeched on the tarmac.

My body's adrenaline response switched from one of anxiety to absolute excitement: 'Fuck me, that was cool! What a rush!'

Glancing around the cabin I noticed a distinct lift in the atmosphere. The demeanour of the passengers had completely changed, most now comfortably chatting with one another rather than talking to God. We taxied to the terminal of Baghdad International Airport (BIAP), which looked remarkably like many others I'd seen around the world. It was a modern, sprawling hub of activity, albeit with one major exception: the overabundance of military aircraft. The usual commercial and cargo jets occupied a number of the departure/arrival gates, but the vast open spaces away from these areas were littered with US Air Force Boeing C-17 strategic airlift transport aircraft and F-15 fighter jets, as well as US Army UH-60 Sikorsky Blackhawks.

'There must be a war going on,' I said to Matt.

'You think?' he said, laughing.

We pulled into our gate and disembarked from the plane, lining up at the customs desk before getting our bags from the carousel. The routine on entering Iraq was similar to that in other airports, but with one major difference: the obligatory US$10 cash payment to corrupt airport officials to ensure a trouble-free passage through customs. The building itself, part of what was formerly known as 'Saddam International Airport', was an impressive one-billion-dollar structure, a monumental piece of architecture apparently designed by Saddam himself that smacked of a 'bigger is better' mindset. Whatever issues Saddam had with size, the airport almost fell into disuse after the first Gulf War of 1991, when the United States and United Kingdom imposed a no-fly zone over Iraqi airspace, severely restricting its use for commercial purposes.

Apart from the bribes we had to pay, things at the airport seemed normal and familiar; there were even a few duty-free shops, and it all seemed to be business as usual. It was hard to believe we'd just arrived in a country caught up in a vicious three-way battle between the opposing Muslim sects and the occupying multinational force headed by the US military.

I picked up my bag from the luggage carousel and followed Matt out of the terminal with a group of other guys who were obviously here for the same reason I was.

'You didn't bring much,' Matt said, noticing I only had my 'war' bag with me—a large military-green multipurpose gear bag I had used in the police.

'Don't need much. It's not like we'll be going out on the piss.'

'Did you bring a jacket? It gets cold at night this time of year.'

'Yep,' I said, unconvinced as I looked up to the sunny sky above.

2

In the Deep End

It was about twenty-five degrees, a pleasant temperature suitable for the cargo pants, T-shirt and running shoes I'd been wearing since leaving Sydney more than twenty-four hours before. Walking into the lower level of a two-storey car park outside the terminal, I noticed a light dusting of fine sand covering almost everything in sight and wondered if a dust storm had just passed through. On the far side of the car park were two large, matt black armoured personnel carriers (APCs) with a number of guys clad in beige uniforms walking around them.

'I've never seen APCs like that before,' I said to Matt.

'They're called Revas, made in South Africa.'

'Why Revas?'

'Apparently it's an acronym for Reliable, Effective, Versatile and Affordable. At least that's what they tell us.'

'Ah, okay then. What's with the V-shaped hull underneath?'

'They're designed to deflect mines and roadside bombs. Hopefully they'll get us safely to the Green Zone.'

'Hopefully?' I said, more than a little concerned.

'Well, we have to travel on Route Irish into the Green Zone.'

'Why do they call it Irish?'

'I don't know. Maybe because, like everything else in this country, the whole thing is backwards. The Yanks give a name to all the main service roads, probably so they can pronounce them.'

Once described by soldiers as 'the most dangerous road in the most dangerous city in the world', Route Irish was the main road connecting the BIAP with the Green Zone and as such had attracted a high number of coalition casualties over the last three years. Route Irish had become the modern equivalent of running the gauntlet— an ancient form of punishment in which a condemned man was stripped to the waist and forced to run between lines of soldiers. As he passed he was beaten or whipped, often with fatal consequences. Matt soon assured me that Route Irish *was* a gauntlet.

'About six months ago a dash-mounted camera captured three contractors getting killed by insurgents when they stopped in traffic on the road,' he said.

'Yeah, I know,' I replied. 'I saw the footage. One of the guys filmed his own death.'

I surprised myself with my matter-of-fact response. I'd only just arrived 'in country' but I already had a sense that life here was just like the duty-free cigarettes and perfume—cheap and easily disposable. With every passing minute it became more and more evident.

'Not a good day out for them, but I suppose the moral to the story is don't stop,' I said.

'You got it, but sometimes that's easier said than done. After all, it is still classified as a normal suburban road. Local Iraqis use it all the time, which makes for an interesting ride.'

'How so?'

'Well, mate, they're still trying to maintain some sort of normality in their lives but the insurgents know this so they load up a car with explosives and try to drive it up as close as they can to any Western vehicles and then detonate it.'

Matt's words hit me like a brick: here I was in a foreign country, under threat from something I couldn't see. I knew I'd need to challenge my preconceived idea of the 'enemy' wearing a black hat while I sported a white one.

'Hey, Horse, this is Rick,' Matt said as we reached the Reva. 'He's the team leader for the trip back to the Green Zone.'

Rick was a stocky, fit-looking bloke of about thirty-five who had a shaved head with a pair of Bollé sunglasses perched on top. He was wearing what appeared to be the stock standard outfit of beige pants, long-sleeved beige shirt and desert-coloured army boots. I shook his hand and looked into his eyes, keen to suss him out. Rick seemed to pass this most primal of body language tests with ease.

'G'day, Rick,' I said, vigorously shaking his hand with a strength that was more than returned.

'Hey, Horse. Welcome to Baggers. Mate, can you handle a belt-fed machine gun? We're a couple of guys short and we'll need someone up in one of the turrets.'

I'd barely been here an hour and I was already being asked to man a machine gun in a war zone! I'd handled large-calibre weapons before but not in situations like this. I was being thrown in at the deep end but the last thing I wanted to do was seem like I couldn't handle it. I couldn't show any fear so I put on the best cool and collected face I could muster.

'No sweat. What type?' I asked.

'It's a PKM. Russian made. Pretty simple to use but I'll give you a quick run-down when you're ready.'

'Cool. We can do it now if you want.'

'Sweet,' Rick said. 'Give me two minutes.'

Rick walked away to attend to other things and, not wanting to sound ignorant, I whispered quietly to Matt, 'What does PKM stand for?'

'Fucked if I know!' Matt laughed. 'It's a bigger version of the AK-47 so it's probably got something to do with that.'

The AK-47 rifle, designed and patented by Russian general Mikhail Kalashnikov in 1947 (hence the name), is still the weapon of choice for military, police and rebel forces in many countries around the world. Its operational longevity, rugged reliability and low-cost availability make it a very popular option in less affluent nations and I was sure there'd be plenty of them floating around Iraq.

As Rick gave me a soldier's five (quick run-down) on

the larger variant of the famous rifle, I began to wonder what I'd just volunteered for.

'We need to keep everyone, including cars, at least two hundred metres from the APC on the way back,' Rick said. 'They should be able to read the signs on the back of the Reva but if they get too close just point at them and put your hand up like a stop sign.'

'What happens if they don't stop?'

'They should, but if not, then fire a burst across the front of the car to scare 'em. We're allowed to do that, but for Christ's sake be careful what you shoot at!'

'Hopefully I won't have to.'

'Mate, we've had some gung-ho fuckwits here who would shoot at anything.'

Over the next few weeks I would quickly learn that the gung-ho fuckwits to whom Rick referred were rife in Iraq. With more than three hundred private security companies operating around the country, most of them under lucrative contracts handed out by the US government to assist the military effort, the lure of wealth had attracted a whole range of guns for hire—wannabe mercenaries from every corner of the globe who'd descended on Iraq to make money for themselves and play soldier at the same time, causing many problems that could have easily been avoided. They were like kids playing war games: some of the boys took it too seriously, while others simply ran about thinking they were invincible, with little regard for anyone else. The contractors in Iraq had a broad mix of experience; they ranged from ex-military Special Forces operators to the average Joe in search of thrills and bragging rights. Under the circumstances, it wasn't that surprising the coalition military took a dim view of these guys. I was now one of them, but I was not willing to become part of the problem.

'Last resort, for me Rick, last resort,' I assured him.

Our hazardous sixteen-kilometre journey along Route Irish to the Green Zone began in earnest after we cleared a massive airport security checkpoint controlling access to the BIAP. The checkpoint itself, a maze of concrete barriers and purpose-built slow points, was designed to allow the coalition soldiers manning it to observe, search and check vehicles coming and going from the BIAP. The T-walls (four-metre-high, one-metre-wide solid concrete barriers) formed a blast-resistant wall surrounding not only the checkpoint but the twenty-kilometre perimeter of the entire airport. Shaped like an inverted 'T', the barriers were put in place individually and then fitted together like a Meccano set.

Jeez, I'd love to have shares in the company that supplies those bad boys, I thought as we cleared the security zone and accelerated onto the open road.

Moving into the 'bad lands' of the Red Zone (a military code name for areas considered unsafe) I could see, from my lofty position in the APC turret, that the surrounding landscape was dry, with the odd green patch here and there that seemed out of place amid the dominant dusty brown. Flourishing date palm plantations, uniformly spaced, lined both sides of the surprisingly pristine dual-lane highway. The plantations and highway gave the impression of a once well-ordered society, although the vast array of dilapidated buildings and burnt-out vehicles quickly belied that.

As for the Iraqi citizens, I could see they were indeed attempting as best they could to get on with their lives under difficult circumstances. Watching the world whistle by through my machine-gun sights I saw families travelling in vehicles and others trying to conduct business at roadside stalls. I also noticed satellite television dishes on the roof of almost every dwelling. I couldn't help but wonder how someone from a Western society would cope with the trauma of warfare in their own backyard. I was fairly certain it would not be like this. I'd had neighbours back home who got upset over an old bloke in a hat driving too slow down the freeway and I couldn't imagine them dealing with a road laden with improvised explosive devices (IEDs). It didn't matter anyway; most developed countries only seem interested in fighting wars in someone else's territory, so the bloke next door would never have to worry about it.

Sitting up on the turret, I thought about how much emphasis we place on trivial things in the West. These people, in comparison, actually had real problems to whinge about, but they just got on with it without kicking up too much of a fuss. When I knew I was going to be coming to Iraq I had begun to think more about the situation here. Just about everyone I'd spoken to had an opinion about the war, but most were relatively uninformed: modern television has certainly seen to that. Every night people are transported into the thick of battle, cheering for their side to win the day, yet in most cases it's the innocent civilians, like the ones I was watching, trying to go about their day-to-day business with some dignity, who are copping it the most.

Within fifteen minutes we entered another maze of T-walls and passed through another checkpoint, complete with M-1 Abrams tanks, and into the Green Zone. Approaching the heart of Baghdad I realised it was actually a pretty good effort for the Iraqis just to keep the city functioning, considering the amount of military ordnance the coalition had dropped during the initial invasion in 2003. Partly demolished buildings with gaping holes where the roofs used to be flanked the route but through my gun sights I looked beyond the superficial damage and began to imagine the former grandeur of this ancient city. In one form or another it had been here for more than five thousand years and these people had one of the oldest civilisations in the world; perhaps their coping mechanism was somehow genetic. This land, at the crossroads of Africa, Asia and Europe, had seen its fair share of wars. I thought about how, apart from the Tigris River, there was nothing here but miles and miles of desert. Tyrants and dictators had come and gone and still these people endured. This country had once been part of the greatest empire in the world; it had been under the boot of foreign invaders; and still the Iraqis endured.

I wondered whether we were just the next in one long line.

Much of the current city had been constructed for the pleasure of a tyrant but it was beautiful nonetheless. Knowing I'd have some downtime before I was deployed,

I was determined to get out and see some of the historical sites and increase my understanding of just where these people were coming from; such knowledge would prove invaluable when my job began. But before I could do that we still had to square away all the formalities.

We turned into a small, dusty street just off one of the main boulevards near the centre of the city, manoeuvred around another T-wall barrier and pulled up in front of a once-abandoned villa that now served as the administration centre for our company in the region. The size of this large two-storey house was enhanced by some shipping containers in the yard that provided storage for weapons and equipment. The street itself accessed the palace complexes of Saddam Hussein and his family; it was disconcertingly quiet and almost completely deserted. Its proximity to the centre of the city meant the villa would have been a prime piece of real estate in its day, but years of neglect and more than a few bullet holes had seriously downgraded its value.

'Talk about your fixer-upper,' I quipped to Matt as I got out of the APC.

'You thinking about investing?'

'Not likely.'

'Didn't think so!' Matt laughed. 'Get your shit squared away and I'll take you on a sightseeing tour.'

'How did you know I wanted to look around?'

He shot me that 'do you think I'm stupid?' look. 'The first thing everybody wants to do when they get here is to look around.'

'Cool.'

After dumping my gear in the nearest room, Matt and I jumped into one of the company 4WDs and headed out for a better look at the legendary city. We drove past the 14th July Bridge, a monument built across the Tigris River to commemorate Iraq's independence from British rule in 1941. I gazed at the arched steel and cement structure and it occurred to me that history has a knack of repeating itself. I had come to Iraq with visions of giving the Iraqi people freedom and democracy, but I couldn't shake the idea that by being here I was, in fact, contributing to the stranglehold of the latest foreign invader. The longer we drove around, the more obvious it became that many of the larger buildings within the city centre had been razed by satellite-guided cruise missiles during the 2003 invasion. However, there was one exception.

'The Yanks left this one intact so they could use it when they got here. It's Saddam's old palace,' Matt informed me. 'We'll go there for lunch when we get back.'

'Oh, I expect nothing less,' I said in a posh voice as I gave a little wave and tried to do my best impression of the Queen.

'Fuck, Horse, you really are a wanker!'

We laughed as Matt pulled into the Al Jundi Al Majhool monument, more commonly known as the Tomb of the Unknown Soldier. We walked toward the disc-shaped monument (which looked like a UFO that had crashed at a forty-five degree angle) and were approached by an Iraqi soldier who had obviously been given caretaker's duty.

'*Salaam Alaykum*,' I said.

'*Alaykum Salaam*,' he replied.

Our greeting, in simple English, means 'hello, peace be with you' and it was my first real attempt at speaking Arabic, having learned a few basics before arriving. I thought it was pretty apt thing for the Iraqis to be saying to one another because God knows peace was something they needed. Although he was a hard-looking man, not that surprising given what he had no doubt been through, I immediately picked up a deep sense of pride in his eyes as he gestured at us, asking to see our identification, unable (or unwilling) to speak English. His hand signals and my rudimentary Arabic were enough to get the message through and he seemed happy enough for us to enter a site that was apparently close to his heart. There was something else that struck me about this soldier's demeanour. The way he carried himself told me he took his menial job very seriously and I wondered if he was a veteran from the Iran–Iraq conflict that had dragged on for most of the 1980s. I wondered how his transition from soldier to caretaker was sitting with him. I imagined it must have been extremely difficult to adjust to his new role serving his country—especially as the monument was completely devoid of anything to guard!

After a brief walk around we went back to the 4WD and drove a short distance to the Hands of Victory monument: two monstrous hands holding matching scimitars that form a dramatic archway at both ends of a 500-metre-long parade ground. Also known as the 'Crossed Swords', it was built by Saddam to commemorate the Iran–Iraq conflict and display his military might. Around the base were thousands of what are reported to be the helmets of killed or captured Iranian soldiers. The once grand parade ground and the monument, unlike the Tomb of the Unknown Soldier, were in a complete state of disrepair. Seen as a symbol of the Saddam era, they had become victims of looters and souvenir hunters, mostly personnel in the coalition forces keen to secure some memorabilia from their time in Iraq. It was a disturbing thought: one country's symbols of pride, all its people stood for and all that made them who they were, taken to another country and put on the mantelpiece or thrown into the wardrobe.

Matt and I parked on the parade ground and walked up the stairs of the grandstand until we were eventually standing in the position where Saddam once stood and inspected his military. I couldn't help but be overwhelmed by the sense of history. It hardened my resolve and determination to know more about this magnificent country.

'Have you been here before?' I asked Matt.

'Yep. Heaps of times. Every newbie wants to come here.'

'I can see why. You can feel the history.'

'I suppose, but I'm not going to get a woody over it. Let's get some lunch.'

'Cool.'

After returning the 4WD to the villa, we walked around the corner and along one of the main boulevards in the centre of Baghdad, dotted every hundred metres or so with reinforced cement blast shelters.

'What's with the blast shelters?'

'Mate, mortars and shit still land in here—that's why

it's not called the Green Zone anymore, because it gave the false impression of being safe. It's now called the International Zone. Go figure.'

'Whatever it's called, it seems safer than that flight we just had!'

We both had a good laugh and continued a few hundred metres further to the front of Saddam's old palace, now being used as the US Embassy. It's a military tactic: occupy the most important buildings in a conquered land to assert control. This building *was* the biggest and best and an obvious sign of power and prestige. Before we walked into the embassy, Matt pointed across the road to a series of portable buildings surrounded by more T-walls.

'That's the PX,' he said.

The Army and Air Force Exchange Service, commonly known as a PX, was a phenomenon peculiar to the American military (a fact I'd gleaned from reading war comic books as a kid). I recognised the joy soldiers got from being able to buy candy and other luxuries during wartime but no comic book could ever prepare me for what I was about to encounter.

'They've got a supermarket, a pizza joint, a post office, coffee shops and, if you can believe it, a Burger King!' Matt informed me.

'You're shitting me?' I said incredulously.

'If we get a chance we'll go to the PX before you head out.'

'That'd be great. I need some shampoo.'

Matt rolled his eyes as he looked at me and laughed, clearly taking in my conspicuous bald head.

The closer we came to the front of the embassy, the more I realised its true magnitude.

'Fuck me, it's big!'

'I get that all the time,' Matt said with a smirk on his face.

'Now who's the wanker?'

'Yep, she is big. You're not going to believe what's inside.'

After going through a security check at the front gate I felt like I had walked through the looking glass. Although the current occupants had not kept the place in the same manner as the previous owner, I had no difficulty imagining the splendour of the grounds in their heyday: velvety grass and ornate fountains in manicured flowerbeds would have stretched as far as the eye could see. Even now, not quite so well kempt, the grounds still resembled those of many European chateaus or palaces.

At first it made no sense but the more I thought about it the more I realised how influential greed can be. I was seeing the extreme. Outside the palace walls people scrounged to scratch out a living but inside was a place created solely for the pleasure of the powerful and privileged. Walking through the main entrance of the palace proper I was struck by the magnificence of the marble, which extended throughout the building as far as I could see. We walked toward the military dining area, once Saddam's grand ballroom, and I noticed gold-coloured trim lining the hallways in every direction. Entering the ballroom I saw hundreds of US soldiers devouring all-you-can-eat buffet meals under the soft light of crystal chandeliers.

Talk about contrast.

'You can get anything you want here. It's ridiculous,' Matt said as he shook his head.

'You're shitting me! Five hundred metres away people are shooting each other and fighting over food scraps and in here we have *this*?'

Although the 'under new management' sign was well and truly posted at the front of the palace, nothing much had really changed. During Saddam's tenure as resident despot, Iraq's citizens had struggled for the basic human needs—food, shelter and water, along with the more modern requirements of power and petrol. Under the new regime nothing appeared different.

'That's not the worst of it,' Matt said, sensing my thoughts. 'Grab something and I'll meet you out the back.'

I was starving and would have been more than happy with a Vegemite sandwich but instead I stood there and contemplated my options. It was truly overwhelming. The menu catered for everybody's tastes: fried chicken, roast meats, steak, bacon, eggs, pizza, burgers, pasta, fries, rice, lasagne, vegetables, salad, ice-cream, cakes, slices, pastries, donuts, bagels, bread, rolls, soft drinks, coffee, cappuccinos, non-fat, low-fat, high-fat, gluten-free, yeast-free, all free . . . the list seemed endless.

I filled a plate with I don't remember what and walked toward a door with a sign reading *Outdoor Eating Area.* I stepped outside and the scene went from ridiculous to entirely obscene. The outdoor eating area was a series of umbrellas next to a pool that wouldn't have been out of place at any number of five-star hotels around the world.

Sitting down to eat, I watched soldiers and contractors swimming like they were at home in their own backyards enjoying a Sunday barbecue. Between mouthfuls of food, I grappled with the surrealism of my surroundings.

'War is hell,' I commented to Matt as he joined me.

'Yeah, mate, it is!' he laughed with equal sarcasm.

When we finished eating we went back to the villa. I grabbed my bags, headed out the front and boarded the Reva for the next leg of the journey to a small academy named Camp Solidarity located on the northern outskirts of Baghdad.

'Thanks for all your help, brother,' I said to Matt before chucking my gear in and boarding the Reva.

'No sweat. Keep safe. See you soon.'

Telling someone to 'keep safe' or to 'keep well' was a throwaway comment in most situations, but in Iraq it somehow took on more meaning, and I knew Matt really meant what he said.

3

Solidarity

Camp Solidarity had recently been established as a learning centre for the Iraqi Ministry of Interior (MOI) to train hand-picked candidates from the ranks of existing military, police and militia to form an elite commando unit. Why it was called 'Solidarity' I will never know. It smacked of wishful thinking; just another one of those wanky military terms or a warm and fuzzy name dreamed up by some politician who hasn't got a clue about what's really going down. Anyway, I had accepted a US Department of Defence contract with a private security company to provide the necessary training, and the magnitude of our task was not lost on me. I knew the guys we were about to train would be vital in restoring some semblance of balance and order to a country which, from what I'd already seen, was in a state of complete chaos. Inevitably the day would come when the coalition forces pulled out of Iraq and then the day-to-day law and order of the country would be in the hands of these guys.

The camp itself was situated near the northern edge of an area known as the Sunni triangle. This imaginary triangle, a large geographical area taking in the whole of Baghdad and surrounding rural areas, was occupied primarily by Sunni Muslims. Under the dictatorship of Saddam Hussein, himself a Sunni, they had enjoyed the benefits of power and privilege. Sunni Muslims occupied the more affluent areas of the country despite the fact that most Iraqis were followers of the Shia faith. Before coming to Iraq I hadn't known there were different Islamic sects; now I learned that the disagreement between the Sunni and Shiite Muslims stemmed back to an argument over who would become their leader following the death of the prophet Mohammed in the year 632. I also found out that, prior to the coalition invasion, the differing Muslim faiths had enjoyed a relatively peaceful time lasting most of the twentieth century, but the deposition of Saddam and the presence of foreign troops had reignited a power struggle that threatened to tear the country apart. Since 2003 the area surrounding the camp had been a hotbed of violence, especially given its proximity to Sadr city—a poor area with high unemployment that was a perfect breeding ground for up-and-coming insurgents.

It was against these insurgents, and in this political environment, that we were to train the new Iraqi police force to fight, and this would all begin at Solidarity. As we drove up towards the camp I was surprised to see that it didn't fit the standard police academy mould. It was an eclectic mix of old buildings surrounded by a thick, five-metre-high solid cement wall dotted with guard towers at equidistant points around the perimeter. It reminded me of a medieval castle ready to repel invaders, and any doubts as to the importance of protection in this security-sensitive area quickly evaporated. Indeed, protection would prove a necessity.

Jumping out of the Reva as it rolled in through the solid metal front gates I grabbed my gear from the storage panniers on the side and simply chucked it down, as I had to help unload all the other equipment and stores. As soon as we'd finished I picked up my sand-covered gear, dusted it off with several hefty slaps, and made my way through the ground floor entrance. The accommodation block had been built during the Iran conflict and was much the same as any dormitory-style accommodation, with a hallway and adjacent rooms. The only difference was the added 'benefit' of blast funnels on the outside of all the windows. The block was three storeys high with the chimney-like funnels running along each level; the funnels were designed to provide protection from glass shrapnel if something nasty was to detonate outside. While I was glad to have their protection, the downside was that they did not allow any vision outside, nor did they let in much light, resulting in a dark, depressing workspace. Added to this, we were only allocated limited space on the lower floor because the floors above were occupied by our Iraqi instructors and the cadets were above them.

'Where do I put this shit?' I asked no one in particular.

'Just chuck it in one of the rooms,' no one in particular replied. 'We'll sort your sleeping arrangements later.'

I threw my gear in the nearest room and headed down the hallway, where I was soon met by a slightly built guy who seemed entirely out of place.

'Are you Horse?' he asked.

'Yep.'

'I'm Fitch, the program manager. Mate, I heard you've done a lot of training coordination before, is that right?'

'Yep.'

Fitch was straight into work mode, no 'Hey, mate, how you going?' or 'Where are you from?'

I'd seen his kind before. Small in stature and personality and surrounded by larger, fit, confident blokes, he was a perfect example of someone suffering from Small Man Syndrome (SMS), masking his insecurities by dispensing with anything that resembled people skills.

'Good, we need a training manager, so you're it. The training schedule in this joint is all to shit, so your help would be fantastic.'

'Yeah, no sweat.'

'Cool . . . by the way, that means you have a meeting with the commandant in about thirty minutes.'

'Ah, okay then.'

'Just remember that we're here to do what the MOI wants, not what he wants.'

I needn't have bothered spending the next thirty minutes trying to unravel Fitch's somewhat cryptic comment. I soon found myself being ushered into a large, garishly decorated office with a bold sign on the door reading *Commandant*. The commandant was a large man with the rank of colonel who graciously welcomed me and provided sweet tea and biscuits as he waxed lyrical about the quality of his academy through an interpreter. Leaning forward with my elbows on my knees, I appeared to be interested in what he was saying, but I couldn't help thinking how much he bore an uncanny resemblance to the previous Iraqi dictator. It made me wonder if Saddam had somehow escaped death and was hiding out as the chieftain of a lowly police academy.

I continued to smile and nod without really listening to his ramblings. I was more interested in trying to assess exactly what kind of man I'd be working with. Experience had taught me that reading the non-verbal cues that make up the majority of our communication was the best way to gauge a man's character. Again, I looked deeply into his eyes. His stature and mannerisms told me he commanded an immense amount of respect. Whether that respect was earned through his achievements as a leader or by the fear he instilled in others I was yet to determine, but one thing was immediately obvious—he was a man to be treated with caution. Although we conversed through an interpreter, no translation was required as the colonel made it abundantly clear through tone of voice and body language that he was very much in control of *his* academy. I respected that we were in *his* country, in *his* area, at *his* academy; however, we were there at the behest of *his* government and as such we had a job to do. I wasn't going to let *him* stand in the way of *me* doing *my* job.

As I continued to observe him, and also the behaviour of some of his lower ranked assistants, it became obvious that the officers who were running the place were still loyal to the ways of the past, preferring the dictatorial 'Godfather' style of maintaining control.

It wasn't a pleasant idea; my job had just become that much tougher. Changes to the training schedule would be met with stringent resistance. I had known from the outset that we'd be pushing shit up hill, but now it seemed our tenuous relationship with the established hierarchy was going to turn into a pissing contest.

A few hours later we were summoned to an opening address by the colonel, at which he introduced me and the other instructors to the cadets. Standing front and centre in a plain-looking hall, he used his large stature and dominant manner to great effect. A deep powerful voice combined with fist-clenching hand gestures left no doubt as to who was in control. Standing on the right side of the room was a line of Iraqi instructors—about eighteen of them—who had been employed by the company to help conduct cadet training, along with a few interpreters and admin staff. Seated in the middle were one hundred or so cadets, and on the left side were the ten expat instructors, mostly Australians, all from either police or military special operations backgrounds, including a number of former Australian Special Air Service (SAS) operators.

Looking around the room, I met with scores of steely gazes. It wasn't as if we were teaching a bunch of fresh-faced rookies; there were strict selection guidelines set down by the MOI and these blokes had been hand-chosen on the basis of their previous experience. Mostly between thirty and forty years old, they'd been around the block a few times, their cynical faces a lot like some of the cranky old senior constables I had worked with in the police—the ones who had stayed in the job about a decade past their use-by date. Many of these guys were tough, hardened veterans of Iraq's long and brutal war with Iran. I would later learn that most of them were Shiite Muslims and had fought on Iran's side in the conflict, but back then I knew very little about the religious politics of the region. This war, instigated after Iraq invaded Iranian territory, lasted eight years, at the heavy cost of half a million lives, and the men who'd fought in it had been exposed to truly horrific violence.

When Saddam Hussein's regime was toppled by coalition forces in 2003, these soldiers had returned home, where some joined the new Iraqi police force, serving as military-style police. They were known as 'commandos' and had earned a fearsome reputation for violent reprisals against Iraq's Sunni community. The commandos had recently been renamed 'special police' by the coalition in an effort to improve their public image, and now they were being retrained to fill a tactical role similar to that of a SWAT unit in Western police agencies—which is why we were there.

I had no doubt the experienced expat instructors would be able to handle these guys but I was not so confident about the local instructors. None of them came from military or police backgrounds and only a few of them had any sort of instructional experience. They ranged in age from twenty to forty-five, and had mostly been employed by our company as trusted friends of people who already worked for the coalition, regardless of where they came from. Though I didn't realise it, some of them were Sunni, and as such had reason to mistrust or fear the commandos and may even have been victimised by them in the past.

The colonel began introducing the local instructors and I watched intently to gauge the cadets' reaction. A distinct air of disdain descended on the room: some of the cadets glared and others blatantly scoffed. I began to wonder whether they considered the local instructors traitors to their country because they were helping the coalition. I also wondered whether they resented being told to listen to people they considered inferior, but as I looked into their cynical faces I felt a sense of empathy. Years before I'd found myself resenting orders given by somebody whom I did not respect; it had been a new experience for me then, but it was an experience I would have again and again, until finally it became a profound pattern running throughout my life. The faces of these Iraqi men mirrored my own frustrations with authority, making the magnitude of the task at hand even clearer. I understood now that we would be climbing Everest. The only consolation was, I hoped, that I could use this shared sense of dislike for my own benefit.

The next few days could only be described as a settling-in period as I adjusted to a diet of ration packs and coffee, due to the company's inability to provide proper meals. A number of the other expats, some of whom had been at the site for more than a month, were beginning to get very annoyed by the constant diet of 'MREs' (meals ready to eat). Although these self-contained meals were a necessity during operations away from base, relying on them for more than a few days always led to frustration among the ranks (especially when it wasn't necessary).

It made little sense. History is full of hungry and frustrated people and there is usually one inevitable conclusion: revolution.

The lack of vision didn't end there. Ironically, even in a war zone, compliance with occupational health and safety rules played a big role in our deployment. Regulations set down by the MOI and US DoD required that I undertake training before I would be permitted to carry and use firearms in Iraq. Although I had extensive experience with many types of firearms as both a user and an instructor— including the M4 assault rifle, MP5 submachine gun, shotguns and various pistols—bureaucracy dictated that boxes needed to be ticked before I could fully invest myself in the training program.

The Solidarity rifle range complex was located outside the academy walls. It was set up and run just like the hundreds of ranges I had been to before, but its location on the banks of the Tigris gave it a surreal feeling. Waiting for the instructors to turn up I sat and watched the wide, fast-flowing waters. They seemed to embody an untapped energy source, an underlying strength just waiting for the right time to emerge. It was late afternoon and the setting sun sparkled on the river's surface. Birds flying overhead slowly flapped their wings as they made their way to their roosts for the night. The view was serene and I felt more at peace with myself than I had in a long time. Lost in the river's majesty, I almost forgot where I was before a tap on the shoulder brought me back to reality.

Turning back towards the firing range I contemplated the paradoxical nature of it all. On the one hand, behind me I had a waterway of such importance that it brought life to the desert, and on the other, I was training with weapons designed to take life away.

The first weapon I needed to qualify on was the Glock 9 mm pistol; no great stretch as I'd won a combat shooting competition with it back in 2002. Predominantly made of synthetic polymers, the pistol was designed and manufactured by Austrian engineer Gaston Glock, and is one of the most popular choices for law enforcement and military units worldwide due to its accuracy, reliability and ease of use. Although a handy weapon to use in law enforcement, the reality was that a 9 mm pistol didn't carry much weight in a war zone; it was a secondary weapon for emergency use only.

The rifle I needed to qualify on was the AMD-65. While the Glock was a lovely, smooth weapon, the AMD was a completely different story. Romanian made, the rifle was a cheap and nasty derivative of the AK-47, chosen by our company to equip our group—another example of their ill-advised penny-pinching. I'd spent many years using the US-made M4 and the brilliantly engineered, German-designed MP5; the AMD-65, in comparison, was a complete and unadulterated piece of rubbish. Its only redeeming feature was that it was chambered to take 7.62 mm short ammunition, which despite the lack of quality of its delivery system would still do the job more effectively than just about any other round in its class. Ignoring my reservations about this means of protection, I ticked the box so I could use it, praying I'd never have to.

When not at the range, most of my time in the early days was spent in my room redesigning the training program so that we could maximise the use of the limited training facilities at our disposal. Compared to many of the rooms in our barracks, the one I had been allocated was almost luxurious.

Almost.

It was barely large enough to fit a bunk bed and a desk, but I was lucky enough to at least have an ensuite bathroom that comprised a basic shower and a squat pan toilet. Very different from the Western-style seating arrangement, using the squat pan was a leg workout in itself as my thighs took my entire body weight as I did the business. Not surprisingly, many of the other instructors had opted to install a crudely constructed toilet seat in the communal toilet at the end of the hall, but I figured, when in Rome . . .

4

The World Game!

In those early days the constant chatter of small arms fire outside the academy walls was a cause for concern as I pondered the possibility of having to defend our position from a determined insurgency, but familiarity breeds complacency and it soon became just another ambient sound, not dissimilar to the clickety-clack noises you hear when living near a railway line. Establishing what was and was not a possible threat became easy. We'd only 'stand to' when the unmistakeable barking of the large-calibre PKM on the roof of our accommodation block shook the whole building. On one such occasion I was jolted from my sleep by a shouting voice in the hallway.

'Stand to! Stand to!'

I rapidly regained consciousness as I heard the PKM screaming above me, throwing out a continual stream of hot lead toward something in the dark. Our Emergency

Action (EA) plan for this eventuality was simple: get our gear on (vest and weapon) and head to the roof. Once up there we'd be better able to deal with the threat. So, putting the EA into practice, we donned our gear and rushed to the roof, only to find that a trigger-happy gunner, apparently spooked by some dark shadows, had let rip, just in case. After the false alarm we prepared to go back to bed. We'd barely reached the top of the stairwell when I heard an AK-47 being fired not more than a few metres behind me.

'Fuck!' I yelled as I instinctively spun around.

Standing among a group of five or six Iraqi academy staff was a very bewildered captain looking down at his smoking rifle. He'd been holding his weapon down by his side when he accidentally discharged it into the cement, very close to the feet of some other guys standing nearby. Luckily, no one was hurt. I probably could have got angry and given the bloke a grilling, but I reconciled it under the 'shit happens' rule.

As I gradually got used to the random gunfire, I set about understanding more about my current environment: where I was, what training the cadets needed and, most importantly, who I'd be working with. Our local Iraqi instructors were a willing bunch of guys, if a little inexperienced, and I greatly admired their courage. For an Iraqi local to provide assistance to the coalition, even though it was purely to provide an income for his family, was seen by many as traitorous. Their departure from the academy on the weekend was conducted with the utmost secrecy to avoid them being targeted by insurgents. Even though the Sunni and Shia sects had a passion for killing each other, they shared an informal unity against the common enemy: the US-led coalition.

Our instructors were an even mix of both Muslim sects and even included one Christian. There were about twenty or so in the group and they had their own hierarchy. The head was an approachable, friendly, surprising young man named Aahil—surprising in that he had an articulate, gentle nature that completely challenged my preconceived ideas about young Iraqi men. These ideas, primarily constructed from the opinions and one-sided reporting of the Western media, were that Iraqis were a bunch of violent ragheads who didn't respect anything or anyone, let alone themselves, a view I could now see was flawed to its core. At the age of twenty-five, Aahil was a qualified lawyer. He was a man whose education and unflappable character would be a great asset to his country if it was ever allowed to move toward autonomy. Because he was the leading Iraqi instructor, developing a sound working relationship with him and the rest of the group would be beneficial for us all.

'Hey, Aahil, do you blokes play football?' I asked during one of our discussions.

'Yes. We love football in Iraq. Very good players here.'

'How about we organise a game between our instructors and yours?'

'You sure you want this? We beat you very easily,' he said confidently.

'In your dreams, sunshine,' I retorted.

'Sunshine? What does sunshine have to do with it?' he replied with a quizzical look on his face.

'Never mind, mate. Let's just organise the game.'

The match would not be played without risk, but injuries or simmering resentments were not our major causes for concern. The football field was located outside the academy confines.

Well inside the Red Zone.

Well inside sniper country.

With one team consisting entirely of white blokes, any half-decent shooter would have a field day, but we figured the risk was worth the reward. Team cohesion was paramount. The threat of a sniper's bullet was all but forgotten over the next few days as we prepared for the match and the good-natured sledging built to a crescendo.

We needn't have worried. Perhaps the thought of the Iraqis beating us on the football field was just as good as knocking one of us off, so the snipers left us alone. The match itself was as unspectacular as it was enjoyable, considering that most of our players had never played soccer and most of the local instructors could not run out of sight on a dark night. For all the shortfalls in the players' skill level, the game was, as far as a team-building exercise goes, a spectacular success. It was our own World Cup as the Iraqi team took on our rest-of-the-world compilation—actually not that dissimilar to what was happening in the country as a whole.

The final score was 3-all.

The teams embraced after the final whistle with a mixture of smiles and laughter but there were many frustrated gestures from the more competitive players.

'We'll have to have a rematch,' I said as I walked back to the safety of the academy with Aahil.

'We will beat you next time.'

'Whatever, Trevor!'

'Who is this Trevor?'

'Never mind, mate! Never mind!'

We both had a good laugh. Perhaps the academy's name was justified after all, but our joy was short-lived and our jubilant mood quickly destroyed. One moment of solidarity was shattered by the dull thud of an extremely large car bomb going off in the direction of Sadr City. I could almost feel the shock waves pass through me as reality hit home and we all came crashing down to Earth.

Over the next few weeks the relationship between the cadets and the instructors deteriorated. The company's decision-making processes and the mandates of the MOI had begun to drive an ever-growing wedge between us. We were refused access to training areas by academy staff, there were increasing complaints about the catering, and the students' participation in physical exercises was lacklustre at best. Their half-hearted efforts were symptomatic of a deeper resentment and with each passing day I sensed it more and more. The cadets' disdain for the Iraqi instructors grew unchecked and the intimidation and threats increased. Our warm welcome was well and truly worn out as the long-established power base in the academy hierarchy was gradually eroded away. I had my suspicions and, as things continued to worsen, it became apparent the commandant was conducting the orchestra. He did not want us to begin training what he no doubt saw as his cadets in his academy. Every time I made a request for materials or suitable training venues he would deny it.

When a specific date for commencement had been set he would issue a public holiday to the cadets. It appeared he would do anything to disrupt and delay our ability to fulfil the training contract.

In all fairness, I felt we needed to take some of the responsibility for the decaying relationship. I'd noticed a couple of expat instructors being particularly disparaging toward the Iraqis, mostly during physical training sessions. I quickly learned that giving out physical punishment in the form of push-ups, a very common disciplinary practice in Western military forces, was a direct assault on an individual's manhood in Iraqi culture, causing them to lose face in the presence of others. The mere act of ordering the punishment was adding fuel to the growing fire. Our ignorance mirrored what was happening around us on a broader scale, highlighting an obvious lack of cultural understanding on the part of the coalition forces.

I remembered back to signs I'd seen at school: 'Bullies only make you feel small so they can feel tall.'

I think, in a perverse kind of way, the coalition was doing the same thing to the Iraqis. Look at what went down at Abu Ghraib prison in Baghdad. Seemingly ordinary American soldiers were caught up in this feeling of superiority over their captives and subjected them to mindless acts of violence and humiliation. Many of the prisoners were tortured or raped repeatedly in a systemic cycle of abuse that apparently didn't ring any moral alarm bells in the minds of the soldiers involved.

It couldn't have. Look at the ridiculous photos they took of themselves smiling and laughing while their victims were in torturous poses. They weren't doing anything wrong. They were superior.

No. They were bullies!

The average soldier is generally not educated to a high level and probably has a chip on his shoulder about his lot in life when he's back home. When his country invades and conquers another, this allows him to feel superior. The longer I stayed in the country the more I began to wonder why the coalition forces had not tried to address this. It seemed pretty simple to me: if you intend to force your will on others and take over their country, then you need to show them goodwill and cultural understanding. You'd think the US would have learned from Vietnam.

Despite the prevalence of testosterone-fuelled madness, there were some decent blokes who seemed to be genuinely trying to make a difference.

One of them was an Australian bloke called AJ, a former SAS trooper, who walked into my office one morning with a broad smirk on his face.

'What do you want, AJ?' I asked.

'Do you know you're nothing but a FOT?' he said.

'What's a FOT?'

'Fucking Orange Thing!'

We both laughed. Although my head was now completely shaven I still had a hint of red hair. In the short time I'd known AJ this was how our conversations generally started. He was an extremely fit, tough-looking hombre whose no-nonsense approach and honesty was refreshing. He definitely came across as a 'say what you mean, mean what you say' kind of guy. I liked that. We had developed a jovial and lighthearted rapport, mostly with me taking the piss out of him for being an Army Jerk (AJ) and him doing the same because I came from the police. Despite the banter, our friendship was based on mutual respect, and we'd often shoot the breeze over a cigar and a coffee at night. It was great to see that a highly trained, uncompromising bloke of his calibre was able to cut through the tough-guy image so prevalent in this industry and just be normal. The mere act of chatting to a like-minded person was a welcome relief—one that might even keep the psychiatrists at bay.

After the obligatory banter, AJ informed me of the reason for his visit.

'Mate, we've got a problem. We were just doing a weapons count at the armoury and there are five Berettas missing.'

'Do we know where they went?'

'I spoke to Haydar and he reckons the commandant has taken them.'

'Why doesn't that surprise me,' I said as I got up from behind my desk.

As if our task of helping to rebuild the country wasn't enough, we were meeting resistance at every turn. This bloke was just making our lives an absolute misery. It now became obvious who was benefiting from the delays.

'All right, I'll see Fitch and we'll see what we can do.'

'Yeah, good luck with that,' AJ said.

I walked into Fitch's office and repeated what AJ had just told me. In the short time I'd known him Fitch had proven to be an inept character, afraid of his own shadow. He was a deadset company man, not willing to challenge authority and certainly not willing to jeopardise his position (or pay cheque) for anyone.

'Okay, I'll email our head office and see what to do,' he said.

'Fuck the email, why don't we just go over there and ask for them back?' I snapped.

'No! We don't want to annoy the colonel!'

'Fitch, we need to sort this now,' I said, trying to seem assertive, rather than angry. 'It really can't wait until you get an email response. Those guns could be in the hands of anybody around here, can't you see that?'

Fitch didn't reply. He didn't know how to. He just shrugged his shoulders and gave me a look that told me he was out of his depth.

Frustrated, but not surprised, I walked back to my own office. I soon found out the Berettas were no longer on academy grounds, and I couldn't get them back, even if I asked. The commandant had apparently given them away as gifts of goodwill to surrounding dignitaries in order to maintain his standing as a chieftain in the community. I had no doubt this had been a common practice for a long time but these weapons had been supplied by the US taxpayer for the exclusive use of the police officers who would graduate from the academy. It grated on me—as did the realisation that the company I worked for was unwilling to make waves, not wanting to jeopardise its multimillion-dollar contracts. It was becoming ever clearer that our welfare, and that of the people under our charge, was secondary to the vast amounts of money being made off the back of the US government.

'Bringing democracy, my arse,' I muttered under my breath.

It seemed to me that this whole country was just one big business opportunity. The coalition wasn't bringing these people democracy and freedom; it was bringing them capitalism and the freedom to make money by exploiting absolutely anyone or anything.

5

Mexican Stand-Off

One morning Haydar, one of our interpreters, knocked on my door while I was lying in bed, rushing in before I could invite him. Ashen-faced and flustered, he stood at the foot of my bed.

'Hi, Haydar. What's up?' I asked, rubbing the sleep from my eyes.

'Mr Shane, I have just overheard something that you must know!'

'What's that, mate?' I said, propping myself on one elbow.

'The cadets are planning to kill all the Australians and us as well!'

'What?'

I was suddenly awake, leaping out of bed and hurriedly putting my pants on. Haydar kept talking.

'I was in the gym and I heard them talking from the floors above. They are going to shoot everyone.'

Strangely, as I've said, the sounds of random gunfire outside the walls of the academy did not interrupt a good night's sleep; however, the constant chatter of the cadets as their voices echoed down the hollow chambers of the blast barriers outside the windows did. Almost instantly my annoyance and frustration at the building's design disappeared; its peculiar engineering was proving invaluable.

Notwithstanding Haydar's excitement, what he was telling me did not really come as a surprise. I'd noticed a shift in the staff and cadets' attitude over the past week or so and even Fitch had decided to do something about it, albeit nothing more than sending an email to the US Army contract liaison officer in Baghdad to complain about the lack of cooperation we were getting from the academy. Now I had a feeling something was really about to go down.

'Do you know when?'

'I think they say tomorrow but I am not sure.'

'Thanks, Haydar. Go and make sure all your guys are okay. Stay calm,' I added, trying to reassure him.

'Mr Shane, I am scared. Many of the cadets are from the Badr Brigade.'

In military and contractor circles there had been a credible rumour circulating that the ranks of the new Iraqi police organisation had been infiltrated by the Badr Brigade—the military wing of the Shiite political party known as the Supreme Council for the Islamic Revolution in Iraq (SCIRI). Many Shiites opposed to the Sunni rule of Saddam Hussein relocated to Iran in the early eighties and took up arms against their fellow Iraqis. After the coalition invasion of Iraq, these self-imposed exiles returned in great numbers to assist in the overthrow of Saddam with the help of their new friends from the West. In 2005, Bayan Jabr, a senior figure in the SCIRI, was appointed the new Minister of Interior of Iraq. As such, he had complete control over the structure of the police force and recruitment of cadets, the result of which was a staggering number of Brigade members changing uniforms to become part of a 'legitimate' organisation. It was rumoured that these new Iraqi police commandos had been responsible for the systematic rounding up of Sunni males, many of whom were subsequently tortured and killed in what could only be described as an act of ethnic cleansing. As I recalled the hardened looks on the faces of the students when I first arrived (and the scared shitless look on Haydar's Sunni face) the rumour seemed to carry a lot of weight.

Not that we hadn't already considered the possibility.

On the occasions when we were required to take the cadets to the range for live fire practice (even though I was sure they had more shooting experience than any of us) we were especially cautious. We had one of our own instructors stand behind the firing line with a locked and loaded AK-47 in case any of these former soldiers decided to take out their frustration on us infidels.

So here I was. I had arrived with noble visions of helping to build a force to oversee the running of the country when the coalition eventually left, but apparently we were doing nothing more than assisting them to commit murder. I'd come here hoping to pass on my knowledge and make Iraq a better place, but the more I learned the more I understood I was, in part, training up the Shia to exact their revenge on the Sunni—a thought that obviously did not sit well. As the pieces of the puzzle slowly came together, I began to realise many of these cadets had been chosen to attend this academy without any background checks or qualifications; they were protected at the highest level by the current crop of powerbrokers, which made their resistance to our training and the intimidation tactics used against our local instructors even easier to understand. A few days earlier, one of the local instructors had been surrounded by a group of cadets outside the meal room while an academy staff member looked on. The instructor's life and his family's lives were threatened because he was now working for the coalition, an incident that scared the shit out of him so much he wouldn't give us any further details for fear of reprisal.

It didn't take long for the message to filter through the expat ranks. Anyone who was away from our area was contacted via radio to bring them back, so we could be prepared as best we could to handle any problems. The last thing we wanted was for any of the instructors, coalition or Iraqi, to be exposed and isolated if something happened. In the following hours we discreetly collected water, food and ammunition supplies from external storage containers. We had to be careful. We didn't want to alert the cadets, or the academy staff for that matter, that we'd got wind of what was going down. With only ten expats and eighteen local instructors versus a hundred cadets and fifty academy staff (all with access to numerous weapons) the chances of us all walking away unscathed in a full-on battle would be slim, and I imagined what Davy Crockett, Jim Bowie and the rest of the guys in the Alamo must have felt like in the days before the Mexican army overran them. We had collected all we'd possibly need for a prolonged stand-off and now we were playing the waiting game, blind to what was going on outside our building courtesy of a company decision to keep everybody inside and out of view. By mid-afternoon an eerie quietness had crept over the academy.

AJ, Fitch and a few others were with me in a hallway, near a stairwell leading to the roof.

'We can't sit here and just wait,' I eventually said. 'We need to see what's going on.'

My words were specifically directed at Fitch.

'Everybody stays put,' Fitch said rather meekly.

'Fuck that shit!' AJ said. 'C'mon, Horsey. We're going to the roof for a look.'

'No sweat, brother.'

Fitch didn't comment; he simply stood there. He was out of his league and he knew it. I read somewhere once that bad leaders are not ones who make bad decisions; bad leaders are ones who don't make *any* decisions. Fitch definitely fitted into the latter category.

I grabbed my AMD and body armour and AJ and I headed up the stairwell with two other guys, Mark and Phil, behind us to take up positions on the second floor so that we weren't so isolated. When AJ and I reached the roof we stepped through the door and out into the unknown, crouching immediately on either side of the doorway and sweeping our weapons in an arc outwards from where we had just come, a standard tactic in which we'd both been trained. Cautiously walking across the roof, we continued to sweep our weapons back and forth as we scanned the ground below, searching for any activity that might give us a clearer picture of what was going down. Suddenly, we heard shouting from the ground floor entrance to our wing and as we watched a stream of cadets poured out into the courtyard, all of them screaming at the top of their lungs in Arabic. I looked over the edge of the building trying to see who or what they were screaming at, but all I saw was more cadets flooding out. I carefully scrutinised the group for weapons but couldn't see any. I made sure the safety catch on my AMD was on and continued to watch as the cadets gathered in the middle of the courtyard, still shouting loudly and gesturing back at the doorway behind them.

'We'll stay up here and provide top cover,' AJ said.

'Top cover?' I mocked. 'You've been watching too many movies, AJ!'

Still unsure what had happened, I looked down again and saw several expats spilling out into the courtyard with the cadets. Their hands flailed wildly as they gestured to the cadets to calm down but nothing was going to settle them. The tension was increasing as tempers and voices reached breaking point, an even mix of Arabic and English making it difficult to tell who was doing the most screaming. From our vantage point the lines between the two groups were decidedly blurred; some of our instructors were mixed in with the crowd. A largely built cadet (who I later discovered was an Iraqi Army veteran) grabbed one of the expats' AMDs and tried to wrestle it from him— an action which could easily have turned the melee into a full-blown firefight if he succeeded. Aiming my AMD at him, I hoped like hell that he wasn't going to get it. I really didn't want to take anyone's life and, considering the shitty aiming capacity of the AMD, there was no way I could guarantee he'd be the only one I'd take out in the process. Over the sights of my weapon I watched them wrestle, waiting and praying I didn't have to shoot. Suddenly I heard a loud siren coming from the direction of the academy gate some one hundred metres away. I couldn't see the gate but I could tell from the reactions below that the cavalry had arrived—and just in the nick of time. Just like in the movies, a US Army Humvee rolled into the courtyard below, sporting a 50-calibre machine gun on its roof turret.

'Never thought I'd be so glad to see the Yanks,' I said, lowering my weapon and looking at AJ. He just smiled but I could see his face was tinged with disappointment. I think he was spoiling for a fight. I'm sure the Iraqis were thinking the same thing but there was no way they were going to take on the might of the American military. Realising the situation was under control, AJ and I made our way back down to ground level.

'What the fuck happened?' I asked one of the other expats as we reached the foyer.

'Mark and Phil followed you up the stairs to go to

the landing on Level 2. When they did, about fifty of the cadets came out of their rooms and started pushing them around. The shit hit the fan so we routed everybody out of their rooms and into the courtyard.'

'Were there any weapons?'

'Yep, they were in their rooms on the beds: a couple of pistols and an AK. We're doing a more thorough room-to-room search now.'

'Where was Fitch?' I asked.

'Hiding in the kitchen.'

'Geez, now why doesn't that come as a shock?'

Fitch didn't just have SMS; he was a small man.

The din settled down but the full scale of the situation's deadly potential became obvious; the cadets had not only the incentive but also the tools to carry out their plans. Mike and Phil's arrival on the second floor had brought the tension to a head before the cadets were ready. I think they would have preferred to wait until nightfall or another time of their choosing but it didn't matter now. It was over. Or so I thought.

Over the next hour or so a stream of people with a vested interest in the academy began to arrive, notably the US military liaison to the MOI as well as the area manager and, of course, all the high-paid hangers-on from the company, no doubt here to protect their investment. We all met in one of the rooms for a debriefing. The area manager was the first to speak.

'Okay, guys, well done. We've had a bit of a chat to everybody and it seems that what you did was in everybody's best interests. No one got hurt.'

Something in his voice told me he couldn't care less about our welfare or that of the cadets—merely the company's contract. It was the most disingenuous bullshit I'd heard in a long time but this was only the start.

'We're just going over to chat to the commandant, so grab a brew and relax. We'll be back soon.'

Thirty minutes later my fears were confirmed. The whole mood changed and the finger-pointing started. I'd seen this type of behaviour before in grown men worried about their livelihood, willing to sacrifice anybody and anything to protect their own arses. We filed back into the briefing room and had barely sat down before the liaison officer, a burly US Army first sergeant, let rip without warning in a broad New York accent.

'You guys are just a bunch of gung-ho contractors! You should be ashamed of yourselves!'

My immediate reaction was 'fuck you'—a sentiment I could see was shared by my colleagues. We all looked at each other incredulously. Not only was this guy way off the mark but he failed to take into account that within the room was over one hundred years of special operations experience in both the police and military, including numerous real-time counterterrorism operations. We knew of many private security contractors who had embarrassed the US military machine on many occasions, but this was not one of those occasions. AJ, never one to take a backward step, said what we were all thinking.

'Were you here, you fuckwit?'

Not accustomed to being spoken to in such a fashion, the bloke went bananas.

'How dare you speak to me like that!'

AJ, given his extensive special operations military experience, refused to back down.

'I'll speak to you however I want to. You're a fucking reservist who's normally a copper in New York, so don't fucking come in here and tell us how to do our jobs!'

I looked at AJ giving it to this bloke and couldn't help but have a giggle at the way he'd worked a jibe at the police into his tirade.

I picked up where AJ left off.

'Weren't you asked to come out here last week because we could see that there was going to be trouble?' I asked. It was a rhetorical question.

'I was busy, but that doesn't matter,' he responded defensively. 'You guys fucked up and there will be an investigation!'

Huffy and still smarting at our response, he stormed out of the room. The area manager also felt like he needed to put in his two cents' worth.

'All of you are being taken back to the villa tomorrow for interviews.'

'Why is this such a big deal?' I asked.

'When we spoke to the commandant he said that the students were forced out of their rooms in their underwear. They were disgraced.'

'We were in the middle of a riot, for fuck's sake!' said Mark.

'Their underwear is a pair of shorts and T-shirt!' said Phil, who'd been with Mark on the second floor at the time. (Much later I learned that this underwear story was only a smokescreen anyway; basically the commandant was trying to cause as much drama as he could.)

'It doesn't matter. The US colonel in charge of private contracts is pissed. He wants to send you to Fort Leavenworth military prison.'

I didn't know whether it was even possible to send an Australian citizen to a US military prison, but it seemed a ridiculous statement all the same.

We were under no illusions as to why they were reacting so inappropriately: the US military was still reeling from the allegations of torture at Abu Ghraib prison and couldn't afford another public relations nightmare. Regardless, it still seemed a stupid conclusion. Notwithstanding cultural differences as to what constitutes underwear, it seemed to me that Phil and Mark had very few options other than to act as they had. They had reacted out of an instinct for self-preservation and their initial decision to order the cadets into the courtyard, backed up by some other guys who ran to their aid, was justified in my mind.

For the next twenty-four hours we were treated like a bunch of misbehaving children, confined to our rooms to appease the commandant. The company was making sure that it was being seen to punish the 'irresponsible contractors' in the eyes of the academy and the military powers that be.

Outwardly, I was angry at the poor treatment being meted out by the company but I secretly felt trapped and alone, restricted to my solitary room, unable to discuss the incident with anyone. I wanted to tell my employers to fuck off but I couldn't, fearful that any deviation from company orders would result in our employment being terminated.

I felt disempowered and disillusioned, overcome by a feeling of helplessness I hadn't really experienced since my wife told me she wanted a divorce a few years earlier. With no apparent choice in the matter and no real ability to express my true feelings for fear of ruining any future with her, I had simply rolled over, taken it and hoped it would go away soon—a schoolboy defence mechanism that hadn't worked then and certainly wasn't working now.

When the Revas finally arrived to take us back to the International Zone, my mood was lifted by the prospect of a reunion with an old mate from back home in Australia. Batman, or Batty as we called him, was a jovial type of guy who didn't take himself, or life, too seriously. Along with Matt, he had done the same counterterrorism selection course as me before the Sydney Olympics and we'd had a close friendship, both in and out of work, ever since. Batty was the one who had encouraged me to come and join him in Iraq, and I was the godfather to his newborn baby boy.

Although I had formed some solid working relationships with most of the guys at Sol, I was looking forward to seeing my old friend again. When finally I saw Batty round the corner of our dormitory block and walk down the hallway it brought on an emotional response I hadn't expected, and I would later find out he had felt the same. He had been in country for many months, and seeing me was like seeing family for the first time. I was overwhelmingly pleased just to see a familiar, trustworthy face after the furore of the previous twenty-four hours. Without words we embraced, giving both our souls a much needed boost. We had probably hugged before during celebrations on the footy field but never like this. I didn't care about the normal 'rules' of manhood; it felt good to reconnect with a good mate after a topsy-turvy couple of days.

It was, however, too brief. In their haste to ensure the old crew of troublemakers did not infect the new arrivals, the company bundled us into the Revas for the return trip to the villa. Batty and I were only able to exchange a brief 'take care, brother' before the doors of the Reva were closed and my tenure at Solidarity was at an end.

Once back at the villa, the interview process was more like a witch hunt than an investigation. With the only evidence of wrongdoing supplied by the commandant, whose obvious motivation was to regain control of his academy, it was evident that one or more of our group would be used as a scapegoat to save the company contract—a punishment which would, in real terms, cost the unfortunate fall guy(s) around $100,000 in lost wages.

In many respects it reminded me of when I was in the fourth grade at school, called to the principal's office to answer false allegations about writing rude notes to a girl in my class. It was a case of being treated as guilty until proven innocent. The principal had placed a heater on the side of the desk I was standing next to so that I was extremely uncomfortable when he spoke to me; it almost felt as if I were being interrogated. Now I was being treated much the same. We sat in isolation in the hallway outside a room, waiting to be called in. One by one we were taken into a room where another former police officer from Australia conducted the short interview, only really interested in where I was when the incident started. After recounting my version of events and confirming that I had been on the roof, I was grudgingly told that I would not be punished for my part in the incident; just the same as when I was a kid.

Others in our group were not so fortunate.

Mark and Phil, the two guys who had originally been set upon by the students on the second floor, were sacked on the spot, essentially because the company believed they were the instigators of the incident. Ordered to leave Baghdad immediately, their departures were hastily arranged and executed.

The powers that be had their scapegoats.

The rest of us were assembled at the villa and told we were going to be redeployed to another site. We were also informed that control of the academy would be handed to the commandant, with the company providing a consultancy-only service. In my opinion, this arrangement would have made more sense in the first place. Instead of the coalition moving in with the intention of changing the training program to fit the Western model, they should have let the Iraqis do it their way. Only time would tell if giving the academy and the country as a whole its autonomy would be the best course of action.

It did confirm one thing: nothing in this place was black and white.

I was extremely disappointed that the company had hung us out to dry, especially after the interviews and formal investigation. After the dust settled it was revealed we had in fact acted in good faith and with suitable restraint; however, we were not permitted to return to Solidarity. As a result, a number of us were driven to Camp Washington airport in central Baghdad to catch a Blackhawk ride down to another company site at An-Numinayah. In effect, despite our innocence, we *were* being banished. Sitting on the Blackhawk I turned to one of the guys as the whirring blades of the chopper began to build up speed.

'What happened to Fitch?' I asked.

'Mate, you wouldn't believe it. He got a cushy job at head office in Dubai.'

'That figures.'

War zones are funny places.

The guys who acted in good faith were punished, and the guys who had failed, out of fear, to do anything before, during or after the event were promoted.

6

The Money Train

The Blackhawk taxied to the take-off area of Camp Washington. My frustration and anger began to disappear as the noise of the chopper's engine increased to a high-pitched whine and we climbed diagonally away from the pad. It was exciting to see this once majestic city from the air in a relatively safe aircraft. With the dramas of the past few days rapidly dissipating, I eagerly peered out of the open door as we climbed to our cruising altitude of about 100 metres. We were flying low at around 250km/h, skimming just over the rooftops and palm trees so that any insurgents would not have time to take aim and fire at us with a rocket-propelled grenade. By the time they heard us we would be over their heads. A few seconds later, we would be gone. The city looked remarkably clean, its troubles buffered by the illusion of distance. Within a couple of minutes we were out over the southern desert, an expansive vista of barren wastelands. Far from being the quintessential desert one might expect, with an endless sea of sand dunes, the terrain looked a lot like Australian outback farming areas in the midst of a drought, with only the odd town or a long, snaking camel train to break the monotony. The thirty-minute flight came to an end when the Blackhawk flared, pitching its nose up slightly to decrease forward movement before touching down at our new base. Situated just outside An-Numinayah, a small town two hours' drive south of Baghdad, the base was a sprawling leviathan encompassing almost twenty-five square kilometres of nothing—a stark contrast to the tight confines of Camp Solidarity. Jumping off the Blackhawk, we walked to a waiting vehicle, where we were met by Matt, the guy I'd arrived on the plane with a mere four weeks earlier.

'Hey, Horse. Welcome to the Num,' he said.

We got into the vehicle, an SUV with police decals on it, and he looked at me with a broad smile.

'So, what happened at Solidarity?'

'Don't ask. I'll tell you later over a beer.'

We drove to the secure compound now being used as the police academy and I noticed many differences to the base I'd just come from; most notably the size. Located within the north-eastern corner of the larger parent base, the compound was more like an academic institution. With four large three-storey accommodation blocks, as well as a separate administration building, it was well equipped to house and educate the 1200 or so cadets who rolled through the facility every three months. Apart from the obvious physical differences, it appeared to be more organised than Solidarity. Cars were lined up neatly in a motor pool opposite the admin building, the area was neat and tidy and guys were dressed in appropriate uniforms—no doubt because Matt had been appointed the program manager.

Unlike the cadets at Solidarity, these new recruits had undergone an official selection process, and had passed the necessary background checks set down by the MOI and US Department of Defense. Even these more stringent security measures weren't enough to stop the corruption, though. Local police generals, knowing how desperate the Iraqi people were to secure steady income for their families, accepted bribes from potential recruits, often after the recruit had pooled their family's entire life savings together just to get on the list of names to be checked by the MOI. Unfortunately, payment of the bribe was not enough to secure a spot in the academy. Some of the guys who had paid with the hope of providing for their family were rejected. No reasons given. No right of appeal. No refunds.

'Horsey, I know you boys had some dramas up in Sol but can you do the training manager's job for me here?'

'Sure, mate.'

'It comes with an air-conditioned office and an extra fifty bucks a day.'

'You had me at hello,' I laughed.

'Cool. Come up to my office when you get your shit sorted.'

'Will do.'

In the days following my appointment as training manager my main task was, obviously, to get out and supervise the training. The schedule had been running successfully for some time so, thankfully, I didn't need to worry too much. Many of the candidates were fresh-faced young men who, until recently, had been goat herders. Already in the middle of their recruit training course, they were being schooled in skills that would eventually help them to provide order and stability when the coalition forces departed.

Despite all the differences with Solidarity, my role as the training manager here was fairly similar, albeit on a much larger scale. With over 1200 cadets, 50 local instructors, 10 interpreters, 5 local admin staff and 20 expats, the day-to-day task of managing the training was a huge one. Our work day began at 5 am with an inspection parade of the local instructors to mark their attendance roll and to give them tasks for the day. Along with the expat instructors they would then head out to various venues around the base to train the cadets, keen to get started so they could finish before the heat of the day really kicked in.

As this daily ritual unfolded in the first few weeks I noticed that the male-dominated culture of Iraq was paradoxical. Outwardly the cadets displayed an overt masculinity, but they were at times extremely effeminate, often holding hands as they walked around the compound. So did some of the local instructors. I just put it down to 'different place, different culture' but one of the expat instructors under my charge, a former Australian Army sergeant, didn't see things in the same light and took a particular dislike to this practice. 'Don't hold hands!' he'd shout during training.

One day he got a bit too full-on so I told him to tone it down.

'Mate, it's a different culture. Go easy.'

'It's fucking wrong. They look like faggots.'

'Would it matter if they were?'

'It's just fucking wrong.'

'Mate, some of the best soldiers in the ancient world were gay. The Sacred Band of Thebes was an elite army of 150 male couples who fought alongside their lovers. Makes the whole mateship bond pretty strong, don't you reckon?'

The sneer on his face showed he didn't agree with my statement, nor was he open-minded enough to accept our cultural differences. He was blinded by the Western way of thinking: men who held hands were gay. I couldn't help but be struck by the hypocrisy of this way of thinking and the more closely I examined it the more bizarre it all seemed. In Australia, the sporting arena is the only place where men are allowed to show emotion in each other's company. Openly crying when you lose a game, patting your mates on the backside when they take a wicket or embracing in joyful celebration when you win a grand final are all accepted forms of male interaction, but only if they occur in sanctioned situations. Hand-holding, it seems, is not acceptable.

This wasn't the only contradiction I had to come to terms with. Who was on which side was also something of a grey area. Watching the training sessions, I began to wonder how many of these students would actually go on to become an effective part of a fully autonomous Iraqi police force and how many would take the easy option and join the insurgency. I'd heard rumours that many of the police we were training were in fact doing work for the insurgency after leaving the academy, being paid US$50 by the people they were theoretically fighting against to plant IEDs near police checkpoints. I have no doubt many were cajoled or threatened with harm if they did not comply. I could only imagine what it would have been like to be stuck in a perpetual cycle of continued poverty, doing whatever was needed to ensure your family's survival, and I soon realised that I was in no position to judge them.

I began to think more and more about the fate of the Iraqi instructors with whom we'd worked at Solidarity so, after a couple of days, I went and spoke to Matt, particularly concerned about how Aahil had fared. Even though I was a small link in a big chain of events, I still felt a sense of responsibility for their welfare.

'Do you know whether any of our instructors from Solidarity are coming here?' I asked Matt.

'Yeah,' he told me. 'We've kept some of them. Some were useless, so we let them go, but we re-employed the good ones.'

'What about Aahil?'

'Yeah, he'll be down in a couple of days.'

I was glad to hear Aahil was to continue his employment with us after the Solidarity debacle but part of me was disappointed for the many others not able to be used here. In the brief time I'd known Aahil and the other Iraqi instructors it had become clear to me that the money they earned with our company, the grand sum of US$350 a month, was vital for their family's survival. After all, apart from joining the insurgency, working for coalition companies was just about the only game in town. The social and economic infrastructure of the country had been all but destroyed and it was only the enormous flow of US dollars pouring in that was keeping everything going.

'Hey, can you meet me in my office in five minutes?' Matt said.

'What's doin'?'

'We have to count a bit of cash.'

When I got to the office I saw Matt with two Iraqi guys who I subsequently found out were the caterers for the student mess hall.

'We just got a shipment of cash in to pay the caterers. We need a couple of senior guys here to watch the count. Do you mind?' Matt asked.

'Yeah, no prob,' I said. 'How much are we talking?'

'Six hundred thousand US.'

'You're shitting me?'

'Nope. Two months' payment.'

I watched the count, trying to appear like I wasn't surprised by the huge pile of money, but one question kept gnawing away at me: how in the hell were they going to get it out of here safely? Minutes later the two Iraqis placed the wads of cash into two large brown paper bags and nonchalantly walked out of the office. I couldn't believe how calm they were! Once outside the base confines they'd be driving around with 600K in an environment not too dissimilar to the Wild West—no doubt with a couple of mates riding shotgun with AK-47s.

'Is that the normal routine?' I asked Matt after the Iraqis left, still incredulous at the whole thing.

'Sometimes it's more, depending on when the cash comes in.'

'So if they're paid 300K per month, how much does the company make?'

'The contract with the US government is for $1.1 million a month. That's just food, then everything's subcontracted to a local caterer for three hundred thousand.'

'You're shitting me! Our company is making 800K a month because the US couldn't be bothered to cut out the middle man.'

'Yep.'

'That's nuts! I wonder what the US taxpayer would think about that one?'

'That's not the worst of it. There are other contracts where the cut is even greater.'

It was becoming increasingly obvious that the huge influx of US money, flown in by the billions on special flights, had created an economy which revolved around the continuation of violence. As long as there was a need for foreign forces in Iraq, American money would continue to flow in to fund the country's restructure. Sadly, many civilians were dependent on this money for their survival. I soon realised that this cycle of dependence would make it very difficult to wean the Iraqi people from the coalition teat.

7

Babylon

Apart from counting random, ridiculous wads of cash, another of my administrative duties was to manage bookings for the firing ranges. The larger base had a number of different live-fire range complexes, each designed for a specific purpose. The pistol and rifle ranges were fairly standard, but the rolling range was a purpose-built facility where APCs, Humvees and other vehicles could be used to engage in range practice that was as close as possible to the real thing: firing live from moving vehicles. The base housed many different units from the US and Iraqi military and these ranges had to be booked in advance so we could accommodate all groups. Booking a range, like everything else in the country, was a convoluted process, and it required attendance at weekly meetings. In one such meeting I was sitting around a table with representatives from various base units. We were listening to the base range manager, an Iraqi captain speaking through an interpreter.

'The rolling range is unavailable on Tuesdays for the next month.'

My eye immediately moved to a US gunnery sergeant who was sitting across from me. His face was etched with a puzzled look as he scanned the room searching for answers. Finding none, he began to speak in a slow southern drawl.

'But . . . we'all use the range on Tuesdays.'

The interpreter relayed what he said to the Iraqi captain. A stern look came across the captain's face.

'Not for the next month!' he said forcefully. He said this through the interpreter, although his conviction was obvious even in Arabic.

The sergeant scanned the room again, completely confused. He desperately tried to find someone to back him up but could do nothing more than repeat himself.

'But . . . we'all use the range on Tuesday.'

Realising he was fighting a losing battle, the sergeant sat back in his chair, folded his arms across his chest and began muttering under his breath. The Iraqi captain had no need for an interpreter. Trying to avoid an incident, a young US lieutenant laid down the law.

'It's not available. Find another day.'

A look of utter despair came over the sergeant's face.

'But . . . we'all use the range on Tuesdays,' he said tamely.

Fucking Yanks, I thought to myself as I watched. I was totally dumbfounded and couldn't help but wonder where they'd got this guy from. Were they all like this, unable to adapt to changing circumstances as they occurred? This was my first real contact with US military personnel, though, so I thought it better to reserve my judgement.

The weeks rolled on and, for the most part, I found that the US soldiers I encountered were a friendly bunch. Our compound ran independently of the larger base and our meal room, the only one on the base serving Western-style food, became a magnet for some US officers, who'd make any excuse to arrive around meal times. In all fairness, though, if the roles were reversed I would have been doing the same thing; an exclusive diet of army-issue ready-made meals was a poor substitute for fresh, hot food.

One day I was eating lunch and chatting to a US Army lieutenant. He shovelled some food into his mouth before coming out with something completely unexpected.

'Hey, do you wanna come out to Babylon tomorrow? We're taking a patrol out in the morning.'

I didn't know how to reply. I really wanted to go but I wasn't sure whether he was only offering because he felt the need to reciprocate for the meal. Either way it didn't matter; the opportunity to walk among the ruins of a once great city was well worth a few meals, particularly when I wasn't paying for them.

Babylon has been referred to as the cradle of civilisation; the fertility of its rich, beautiful lands is the result of its position between the mighty Tigris and Euphrates rivers. As the jewel in the crown of ancient Mesopotamia (a name derived from Greek, literally meaning 'between two rivers'), it was a thriving metropolis that gave birth to commerce, science, mathematics and all things modern, but these desirable traits also made it a perpetual magnet for conquest, control and violence.

Given the history of the place—and the fact that the next day was a rest day—I was keen to go.

'Mate, I'd love to. What time are you going?'

'About 5 am. We have to get up before the guys who set the IEDs.'

The IED had rapidly become the most popular weapon in the insurgents' arsenal. Beginning as rudimentary devices resembling homemade bombs, they'd progressed to be as intricate in design as they were deadly, accounting for over half the coalition casualties since the conflict began. Its latest variant, the explosively formed penetrator (EFPIED), had proven an extremely dangerous and highly effective killing tool, its molten copper arrow capable of penetrating even the thickest of tank armour. Even worse, it was often able to be activated by more sophisticated stand-off methods such as remote control or the tripping of infra-red beams.

'Sweet,' I said. 'I'll meet you out the front of our compound at five.'

However, nothing in Iraq stayed secret for very long and word got out about my impending field trip. Matt approached me in the hallway of the admin building later that day.

'Hey, Horse, I hear you've been asked to go to Babylon tomorrow?'

'Yes, mate, heading out at five!' I said, excited.

'Sorry, dude, you can't go.'

Having built my hopes up, I was far from happy.

'Fuck off . . . why not?'

'It's too dangerous. The company would kick my arse if I let you go.'

Although I knew Matt was the furthest thing from a company man I also knew he'd be placed in an awkward position if he did let me go. I greatly respected him so I reluctantly agreed with his decision.

'Fair enough, mate. I'll tell the Yanks I'm out.'

It turned out Matt's caution was justified. The next day another US military convoy was hit by an EFPIED just outside the base, resulting in the tragic death of a US soldier.

Unable to leave the base for any reason, I felt stifled, and day-to-day life could have become very monotonous, save for a well-equipped gym that we set up and a bar in one of the abandoned blocks. Our base was classified as 'dry' but as Australians we felt almost duty-bound to disregard the rules and let off some steam over a drink. Our Thursday night sessions, complete with catered barbecue dinner, became a highlight of the week; Friday was a rest day because it was the Muslim Sabbath. These sessions were conducted away from the eyes and ears of the students, to respect their faith, but we had many nights of singing, trivia and drinking. Regrettably, though, as is often the case, stupidity and alcohol can make for a dangerous mix.

On one particular night I was talking with Matt and a visitor to our bar, a US Air Force lieutenant colonel who was the security supervisor for the parent base. An intelligent, thoughtful man who'd transferred to the Air Force from

Army Special Forces, he did a lot to dispel the opinion I'd begun to form about the US military. Our conversation was intermittently interrupted by a succession of loud noises in the background; a few of the other expats were a bit rowdy after a few too many drinks and were throwing something at the dartboard on the wall opposite the bar. We continued chatting, trying to ignore the uproar, when an AK-47 bayonet landed at the lieutenant colonel's feet, having bounced off the dartboard and rebounded about fifteen feet back to where we were standing.

'Pull your head in, Tonka,' I shouted across the room.

'It wasn't me!' he argued.

I looked at him in sheer disbelief. Here he was, a grown man of forty-five, acting like a five-year-old who swore blind through a full mouth, with crumbs on his lips and his hand caught in the cookie jar, that he hadn't taken a cookie.

'It was you, idiot! Grow up!'

Tonka was the type of bloke who gave contractors a bad name. He'd been in the Australian Army as a regular soldier and only got the gig in Iraq on account of a friendship with one of the managers in Dubai, proving nepotism was alive and well. Extremely overweight (hence the name Tonka), he was a definite liability, especially if the shit hit the fan.

'Sorry about that,' I said to the lieutenant colonel as I turned back to our group.

'Yeah, no worries. We've got them too.'

Yeah, too right you do, I thought to myself. *It's a shame there aren't more like you.*

Ten minutes later, Tonka was at it again. This time, not wanting to walk the twenty or so metres to the nearest toilet, he decided it was a better idea to urinate on the floor where he was standing. Unfortunately, the floor had smooth tiles which caused the urine to splash over both my foot and our visitor's.

'Fuck off!' I shouted at him, embarrassed that the lieutenant colonel copped the spray as well.

Tonka hurriedly tried to put his dick back into his pants while I grabbed him and pushed him out into the hallway. It reminded me of the nights I'd spent as a nightclub doorman in my youth. In my younger days, I would have belted him, but I guess I was starting to mellow. Though I was furious, I calmed myself before I spoke and gestured to the open door.

'Get out!' I said firmly.

It was short and sweet but the message got through and he walked out without a word.

It was not my job to lecture a man older than myself about the rights and wrongs of drinking, nor was it my responsibility to take the law into my own hands. After all, I'd been drunk several times since I'd been here. What was disturbing was that good blokes like Aahil, and a great many other Iraqis, were forced to listen to a tosser like Tonka—a recipe I was sure was being repeated all over the country. The coalition had come here to sell the benefits of democracy to a country that had spent decades under a dictatorship; but they were not exactly presenting themselves as role models, and nor were some of the Australian contractors.

Back in the bar I once again apologised to the lieutenant colonel.

'Sorry about that . . . again.'

'No sweat, Horse. I've seen it all before.'

That short statement summed up something I'd been thinking about since my arrival. The blokes who'd been around the block and seen a few things were the best ones to work with. Blokes like Matt and AJ and another couple of special forces guys who worked with us were never flustered no matter what was happening, always keeping their heads when something was going on.

When we weren't partaking in a few relaxing Thursday night drinks, the gym occupied most of our downtime. With little else to do, afternoon stints on the equipment became habitual, while others found solace running around the vast network of dirt roads within the base's perimeter fence. I'd once been a keen runner but my large build and many miles of training over the past ten years had resulted in knees that screamed every time I ran more than a few hundred metres. Some of the guys had attempted to cajole me out onto the perimeter fence track, to which I had a standard reply: 'You can't flex cardio at the pub!'

During one of the gym sessions one of the expats came up to me.

'Have you tried steroids, Horsey?'

'No, brother—why, have you got some?'

'No, but I can get whatever you want.'

'Where?'

'I have a local contact who can get us anything on the black market. Deca, Dianabol, Stan.'

'What do you reckon?' I asked, not knowing a lot about steroids, never having really considered taking them.

'I'd go with Deca. It's the popular choice here. Nearly everyone I know is on it.'

I wasn't that surprised. With very little else to do, money to burn and nothing to spend it on, it seemed like a viable, if slightly dishonest, option.

'Do I have to inject it or can I take it orally?'

'Inject.'

'I hate needles. Are there any I can take as tablets?' I said, showing my naivety on the subject.

'You can take D-Bol but you'll need to get some other stuff to take with it, otherwise you'll get bitch tits.'

I'd spent enough time in the gym to know exactly what he was referring to. Some steroids, including Dianabol, can cause the body's natural hormone levels to become unbalanced, especially when taken in high doses. When the body is getting that much external male testosterone, it basically says, 'Hey . . . I'm getting enough, so I'll stop producing my own.' This allows the normally dormant female hormone, oestrogen, to kick in, which can result in the development of *gynecomastia*, more commonly known as 'bitch tits'.

'Fuck that,' I said. 'I'll take the Deca.'

A couple of days later a few vials of Deca-Durabolin arrived and I began my first course of injections, almost sick as I prepared to stick the needle into my thigh. I continued to inject every second day for the next two weeks. I could feel a difference in the way my body reacted to my daily workouts, but this euphoria was not to last.

One afternoon I was doing a series of chin-ups when I felt a pain in my left shoulder blade akin to getting stabbed in the back. Having trained for many years, picking up a good number of injuries along the way, I didn't think much of this one, believing it to be a mild muscle strain. I couldn't have been more wrong. It started out as a dull pain but I quickly discovered that I was unable to walk or stand with my hands by my side, only finding comfort by holding my left hand on my head. It must have been a funny sight, me walking around everywhere with my hand on my head, even at mealtimes, but it was the only means of relief. The injury also made for sleepless nights.

Three days had passed and I was still in a bad way when Aahil, freshly arrived from Camp Solidarity, saw my predicament and offered to work on the area to try to alleviate the pain.

'I can do massage,' he said.

'I thought you were a lawyer,' I said.

'I am but I also do massage course.'

Willing to try anything to get the pain to subside I agreed. After the training day had been completed, Aahil came over to the common room in my accommodation block to manipulate and massage my shoulder blade. At first I thought it might be a bit weird having a massage from an Iraqi guy but then I recalled how many times I'd been treated by a male physiotherapist when I had been injured playing sport. It was no different really and I could not deny the results—an incredible improvement in mobility and significant pain relief after only a couple of afternoons.

I was grateful and wanted to do something for him in return. 'What size shoe are you, Aahil?' I asked him.

'I don't know. This size?' he replied, thrusting his right foot out in bewilderment.

'If these fit you, would you like to have them?'

I showed him a pair of Merrell hiking shoes I'd bought just before coming to the Middle East. They were near new, and had cost me about $200, but the price seemed irrelevant considering the help he'd given me.

'No. I cannot take them. They are yours.'

'Aahil, I can buy heaps of these when I leave. You may not be able to. Please take them as a gift; it's my way of saying thank you.'

I could see by the look on Aahil's face that he was totally taken aback by my small act of gratitude. I'd seen so many locals struggling to make enough money for their families, working hard in return for very little, and I was more than happy to give away something I didn't even wear that much.

'Thank you,' he said, smiling broadly as he took the shoes.

The pain subsided over the next few weeks and I could now walk around normally, thanks to Aahil's work. However, I soon discovered all the strength in my left arm had disappeared and I was unable to do even a single push-up. The injury had caused the nerve running down the back of my arm to completely shut off. Watching me try in vain to do anything with my left arm became a source of amusement for the boys and my nickname soon changed from 'Horse' to 'Gimp Boy'. Although I was rather frustrated I still managed to see the funny side.

Unable to kill time in the gym I began to think more about what I was doing and started to wonder why I'd had the desire to experiment with steroids in the first place. Was it merely to keep fit or were there deeper reasons? Perhaps I was trying to maintain an image of strength in an adrenaline-fuelled and hyper-masculine working environment. Whatever the reason, my body was definitely telling me that my brief experiment with steroids was a complete disaster.

Not long after this, there was an incident that showed me I had gained Aahil's trust—but it also saw me lose all faith in my employers. During a training exercise at an abandoned village used to simulate building assaults, Aahil approached me and said, 'Hey, Horse. Can I talk to you?' I'd asked him to call me by my nickname, not wishing to appear aloof or better than him or the other instructors.

'No sweat, Aahil. What's up?'

'Some of the students have told me that one of your instructors is watching them when they go to the toilet.'

'What? Who?' I said, half knowing who he was talking about.

'Mr Clint. Every time they go for a piss behind the building he goes to watch them while he smokes his pipe.'

The instructor to whom they were referring was a strange cookie. Ever since he'd arrived at the base, courtesy of a close friendship with Wally, the executive program manager, and a company director in Dubai, he'd alienated just about everybody. Although appearances are not the measure of a man, Clint certainly seemed out of place in this harsh environment. About fifty-five, unfit and overweight, he really stood out among a group of guys who maintained a certain level of fitness as a result of their tactical policing and military backgrounds. I'd always prided myself on being open to others and accepting them for who they were but Clint severely tested this practice. He was a pompous, pipe-smoking know-it-all. He was never short of an opinion during conversation at the dinner table nor was he shy to pass judgement on others around him. He reminded me of British Army officers from bygone eras who treated those around them with contempt if they were not of the same class, especially the local people in regions they had just conquered. Clint assumed a superior air in front of the Iraqis and also the expats, even putting on what sounded like a fake posh accent to complete the charade.

From what Aahil was telling me now it was entirely possible my reservations about Clint were well founded.

'Does he do anything?' I asked.

'No, he just watches them.'

'Okay. I'll see what I can do about it.'

When I told Matt what Aahil had told me I could tell I'd just put him in another awkward position. He knew about Clint's connections to the hierarchy in Dubai and so would have to handle the matter with a delicate touch. However, in my view there was no grey area. We had a responsibility to the cadets, especially the younger, more impressionable ones. Even if the allegation proved false— and in all honesty, apart from the say-so of some of the cadets, there was very little evidence to support it—Clint shouldn't be spared questioning based on his association with friends in high places.

The day after I informed Matt of the allegations he called me into his office.

'Horsey, Dubai doesn't want to do anything.'

'What do we do then?'

'We'll move him to a position that keeps him away from the cadets. It's the best we can do.'

This response from Dubai was the latest in a long line of mind-boggling decisions made by the company over the past few months. The manner in which the company conducted its business was not surprising, given it was founded and run by former tactical operators from the Australian police, but I was beginning to understand that the self-serving, ego-driven nature of people attracted to this kind of work did not necessarily make them good businessmen—or even more importantly, good managers.

8

Arming the Insurgents

The following weeks rolled into months. Our focus on day-to-day training changed to preparing the students for graduation. It was a very security-conscious affair, a highly political event, resplendent with visiting dignitaries from the MOI as well as a two-star US Army General. Not only did we have to consider the welfare of more than a thousand students, but also the safety of the dignitaries. The logistics were quite staggering.

With the aid of our mate from the bar, the lieutenant colonel, our management team developed the necessary strategy for the event. As a part of this, Wally prepared a set of operational orders and delivered them on the evening before the graduation; he also set out the individual responsibilities for the following day. I had given and received 'OP orders' on numerous occasions but these were by far the worst I'd ever witnessed or heard.

OP orders should be succinct. Only the details relating to the actual operation should be relayed, so the individuals concerned are clear on their role. If you clutter the whole thing with superfluous information the possibility of making mistakes climbs exponentially. OP orders usually take a maximum of about thirty minutes; this set took about two hours.

I sat there with many of the other expats and I couldn't help but notice how their concentration began to drift. Since Wally's arrival a few weeks earlier, he'd proven himself an autocratic 'do as I say not as I do' type of leader—in other words, he wasn't one. Looking around the room I noticed that those still awake seemed bored. Even the lieutenant colonel had fallen asleep. An orders group is normally followed by a question-and-answer session, so that any misunderstandings can be cleared up. In this instance everybody, bar none, couldn't wait to get out of the room.

As we walked out, Brett, a vastly experienced former SAS trooper, said, 'That bloke is a deadset fuckwit.'

The orders proved to be as useless as a chocolate frying pan. Amid all the pomp and ceremony there were several mishaps arising from the ambiguous orders. In one instance a group of students assembled on the wrong side of a gate, directly violating Wally's orders. I headed over to the gate and spoke to another expat instructor about it before deciding that we'd leave them where they were. It had no bearing on the graduation's outcome, so there was no point putting them back through the gate only to have them come through again ten minutes later. When Wally came over and saw that his orders had not been followed to the letter, he went ballistic.

'Horse!' he yelled, patting the top of his head in the universal army hand signal for 'come to me'.

'I'm just here. You could have just asked me to come over,' I said.

'Everything has been fucked up!' he screamed.

'There's nothing wrong here. Some guys went through the gate. Big deal.'

'That's not what was in the orders!'

'If you want to have a discussion about it, I don't think this is the time nor place.'

'I'll talk to you when and how I want.'

Given his liking for hand gestures I didn't bother to reply. I simply turned, gave him the 'talk to the hand' gesture and then walked away, knowing that to listen any longer would result in me dropping him. This wasn't the place or the time to be taking out personal frustrations, either. We still had to coordinate the movement of a thousand or so cadets onto trucks, each with an armed military escort for the perilous trip back to Baghdad. It was a complete nightmare.

All of the cadets had to be individually issued with an AK-47, ammunition and all the other equipment they'd need for the trip and for their new position in the police force—but it was an exercise in futility. I'd observed corruption and the theft of equipment first hand at Camp Solidarity; I'd also heard that when the students arrived at their allocated station, most of their issued equipment, including the AK-47s, would be taken by the local commander for his own benefit. Ironically, they were often sold to the insurgency.

So here we were, in effect, arming the insurgents.

I'd previously heard that during the initial coalition invasion, the Iraqi Army was issued with only two rounds per soldier. Knowing they had little chance of securing victory or successfully repelling the invaders, some local generals went around and collected one round from each of their soldiers so they could then sell the ammunition on the black market for a tidy profit. Sadly, as I came to hear more and more about superiors stealing from their subordinates, it surprised me less and less. It did seem to explain how the invasion was completed so quickly, with very few coalition lives lost to enemy action. Although these practices were well and truly in place before the occupation, it now seemed that the systemic corruption was being fuelled by the exorbitant amounts of cash floating around.

Shortly after the cadets were safely out of our compound and on their way to new careers, Wally approached me.

'Hey, Horse, I wasn't having a go at you earlier.'

'Bullshit,' I replied.

'I was just pissed off because that was the third mistake for the day. They should know better.'

'Mate, most of them weren't sure what was going on, so they improvised.'

'If they weren't sure they should have taken notes at the briefing. These guys are all experienced tactical operators.'

'I agree, to a point, but ultimately we have to take responsibility.'

'What?'

'Mate, we're the ones in leadership roles. It's our responsibility to make sure we communicate properly.'

I tried to talk to him calmly, to treat him like a normal human being, and, for a moment, he looked calm enough to have a rational conversation. Then his real personality re-emerged.

'No fucking way!' he barked, before storming off toward the admin building.

I knew I'd just made a dangerous, well-connected enemy. He'd gotten his position by virtue of his friendship with the company's operational manager in Dubai, a guy whose job it was to hire and fire. Knowing this, I figured my tenure was going to be much shorter than expected.

The day after graduation Matt addressed us at our regular 5 pm briefing—a daily occurrence, intended to keep us up to date with what was going on around us. These briefings made it obvious, at least to me, that what was going on in Iraq was not filtering out to the rest of the world. Back at home in Australia I'd had no idea of the full horror. Just about every day we were informed of the harsh reality of just how many people were being killed; dead bodies were literally turning up everywhere. They were found floating in the river, lying in the streets and piled at rubbish dumps, usually in groups of five to ten, often male, always tortured, mainly the victims of sectarian violence. These horrendous events were rarely reported by the media, who were only interested in more newsworthy items, like large car bombs with multiple casualties.

Normally Matt would supply information and statistics relating to insurgent activity in the previous twenty-four hours, but today he had little to say.

'The company has lost the training contract here at Num. As a result we have to cut some guys. They leave next week.'

It seemed I didn't have to wait for the results of my run-in with Wally. We were all losing our jobs anyway.

'Everyone will be leaving eventually but the guys who are leaving first will be worked out in the next few days,' Matt added.

'What happened to the contract?' one of the others asked.

'Don't know, the company won't say.'

The announcement didn't surprise me.

'Our individual contracts are up in a few weeks anyway. Can't they wait?' I asked.

'Apparently not. I'm sorry.'

The room quickly filled with an atmosphere of resentment and anger. Many guys were severely pissed off with the company already, due to short cuts taken in training and safety. Their frustrations now bubbled to the surface and they began to voice their anger.

'Those pricks in Dubai are cutting people on the ground so they can keep up their lifestyle, aren't they?' one expat asked.

'I don't know,' Matt said diplomatically.

Another guy answered the first guy's question.

'Well, I do. I know they have whores on the books in Dubai. They've got prostitutes on the staff as paid employees so they can get their rocks off and then they cut our numbers. Pricks!'

The groundswell of anger was difficult to quell. I was in a leadership position but I also felt betrayed by a company that appeared to be interested only in profit, personal pleasure and jobs for the boys.

Whichever way the employment axe fell, I'd only have to put up with things for a short while longer. Within a couple of days the decision on who was to leave was reached. In fact, some of the outcasts chose to go before they were pushed.

9

Noises in the Dark

'Now that's a fire,' I said to myself as I stood alone in the darkness, marvelling at the dancing flames. They glowed like an amber beacon against the desolate, pitch-black countryside. Entranced by the flickering light I was reminded of childhood camping trips, and pondered the strange peace of this moment, so distinct from the endless violence around me.

I sucked back on the numbing pleasure of a cigarette. I liked the name, Gauloises—a brand whose slogan, *Liberté toujours* (freedom forever), had allegedly persuaded luminaries such as John Lennon and Pablo Picasso to smoke them, giving me an illusory feeling of sophistication amid the death and destruction. In reality, though, the greatest pleasure I got from this brand was the fact that they only cost US$5 per ten-packet carton.

The more you smoke, the more you save, I thought, chuckling at the absurdity of the idea.

I basked in the solitude, knowing my departure from the shit fight that had become my Iraq experience was imminent. I periodically stoked the fire with papers containing confidential personal information about me, gathered over the previous seven months. The destruction of these documents would ensure that my details could not be gathered and used by a determined insurgency, but more importantly it was a symbolic cleansing of my psyche, an act of moving away from a vocation I was now beginning to realise did not serve my purposes anymore. I sat contemplating my impending escape when, suddenly, a distant whistling penetrated the night air.

I've heard that noise before, I thought. *It sounds like the rocket noise they use in cartoons.*

The noise grew louder as I dismissed thoughts of the Road Runner battling with Wile E. Coyote and I suddenly had a reality check; the sound was more likely something much more sinister. Seconds later there was a loud explosion as mortar shells began to rain down in the vacant area of the compound about 200 metres from where I was standing. Mortar attacks had become a very common tactic against coalition forces. Able to be launched from a distance, they guaranteed a certain level of anonymity for the firer. Their use—or misuse, depending on your perspective—had been one of the major reasons for the name of the Green Zone being changed to the International Zone, after this allegedly safe area became the target of many a well-directed mortar. The noise of the explosions died down, replaced quickly by the scream of warning sirens. I could see a large plume of smoke and huge amounts of debris had been kicked up. I turned back toward the fire, added some more papers and drew back deeply on another Gauloises.

It's a long way away, I thought, but about thirty seconds later the whistling noise pierced the darkness once again. Something was different—the noise was growing louder, and travelling in a different direction . . . it was travelling in *my* direction. Rapidly shaking off my air of nonchalance, I quickly looked around and, not knowing where to go, had to trust my instincts. 'Fuck me!' I yelled, and ran for the cover of a nearby wall.

The noise grew into an ominous scream as I threw myself face first into the dirt like a baseball runner stealing home, covering my ears and fearing the worst. In that moment of terror a feeling of complete calm washed over me and I entered a dreamlike state in which time seemed to stand still. I'd experienced moments like this before, watching as my body, placed under great duress, triggered a primeval response system that acted as a defence. As I lay in the dirt a crazy mix of images, thoughts and questions began scrolling through my mind, beginning with the most fundamental question: *what the fuck am I doing here?* Only now did I realise that the disenchantment I'd been experiencing for several years prior—at times bordering on indifference—was merely a signal for me to take a good look at who I was and how I wanted to live my life. I'd been doing this kind of work for many years, and the actions of the company didn't surprise me—I'd had similar experiences in previous jobs—but somehow it had allowed me to see more clearly what I didn't want. It was a great starting point to begin working out what I really did want my life to look like.

A deafening explosion rocked the ground not more than twenty metres from where I was lying, jolting me back to the present. Small pieces of rubble and debris began to land on and around me, turning the area into a dust bowl and adding to my already heightened sense of uncertainty. The howl of emergency sirens once again penetrated the serene night air. I quickly got to my feet and made a beeline for my accommodation block, checking I still owned all of my body parts (particularly the ones between my legs). I entered the barracks and turned to see the fading glow from my fire, smiling as I thought, *Geez, I'm good at making fires!*

Watching the fire I realised its metaphorical significance: the old Horse was dying. In the safety of the accommodation block I lit another cigarette, leant with my back against a sandbag wall and began thinking back to how the old Horse had been born.

10

Selection

Driving to Holsworthy Army Barracks in October 1999 I had a good sense of what was in store. My mouth became desert dry and my stomach started to twist. Visions of pain, suffering and mental torture played over and over again in my head, as did the question: *What the hell am I doing here?*

My anxiety only increased as I reached the front gates and the security guard came out to check my ID. Satisfied, he pushed the button to lift the boom and, as it lowered behind me, it brought down with it familiar feelings of unease.

The NSW Police Tactical Operations Unit or TOU is a special operations response team—what members of the public would generally call a 'SWAT team', even though 'SWAT' is an American term, not used by state or federal police anywhere in Australia. It had been my ambition to become part of the TOU since watching some darkly clad guys jump out of a van during a drug bust in a McDonald's car park in Sydney's eastern suburbs when I was a probationary constable. The scene seemed like it was straight out of movie: all submachine guns and balaclavas as the team overwhelmed the offenders. I liked what I saw. It appealed to the little boy inside me who wanted to run around with a big gun and prove I was one tough hombre to all and sundry: the pinnacle of what I thought it was to be a man.

I desperately wanted to be part of the TOU, and this selection course was designed to identify prospective operators to become a part of the unit's Sydney Olympics counterterrorist (CT) project.

It was early morning and the sun was barely up.

I checked my watch; it read 5.45 am.

Orders received prior to this point required us to be standing on the parade ground at 6 am. I pulled into the base car park set aside for our vehicles and forced myself to drink the last drops from a large bottle of water. Experience told me what to expect: the ultimate test of physical and mental strength over the next seven days.

Still with both hands firmly grasping the steering wheel I took one last deep breath and tried to collect my thoughts. Try as I might I couldn't shake the self-doubt. They hadn't picked me before so why was I back here? What was it that I needed to prove?

My last attempt at this course had not ended well. Although I completed the entire program, the selectors had decided there were better candidates for the few positions available. In all fairness, I struggled through some of the exercises and there were some extremely fit blokes who I knew had outshone my efforts. I wasn't that surprised not to be selected but it was ego-shattering news nevertheless.

'You can come back next year if you like,' they told me at the time.

Struggling to hold back tears, I told myself not to cry. If I did it was a clear sign of weakness. I choked down the disappointment, but right then the thought of coming back for another seven days of torture was the furthest thing from my mind.

I had failed, and for the next six or so years the demons of defeat ate away at my soul, but something had brought me back to put myself through the punishment all over again.

Here I was, thirty years old and not as fit as I had been on the last course due to some lingering leg injuries that had plagued my preparation. Unable to run quickly, I restricted my lead-up training to slow ten-kilometre runs with a thirty-kilogram pack on my back—that and a few thousand mandatory push-ups. During this training, as I traversed more and more lonely miles, one question kept repeating over and over in my mind: *What the hell am I doing this for?*

I made my way from the car and into a vacant lot where I saw a group of hopefuls already lined up in formation. Walking to an available spot in the ranks I saw a few familiar faces in the crowd but this was not the time for chitchat as the course instructors appeared and began to circle the group like a pack of hungry lions stalking their prey. I looked around carefully, not wanting to draw attention to myself with any obvious movements, and mentally counted how many guys had signed up for this torture: about thirty or so, give or take.

'Get over here, you maggots! Run!' one of the instructors yelled at a couple of guys who had arrived just after me.

And so it began. From now on, walking anywhere was no longer an option.

Once everybody was in parade formation our uniforms were subjected to inspection.

'Everybody hand over their watches,' one of the circling instructors ordered.

Those who were wearing watches removed them and, while they tried to remain stern-faced, I could see they were wondering why the instructors were taking their timepieces. I knew full well. Time gives structure to our days. It gives us a sense of routine and it can be very disconcerting when it's taken away. Not knowing what time it is—and hence when you can expect to finish a task—makes you anxious. Confiscating the candidates' watches was a way of accelerating this anxiety and testing our mental strength.

'Did you iron that with a brick?' I heard one of the instructors scream at a randomly picked candidate.

'No, staff!' he replied loudly.

'Well, it fucking looks like it! If your shirt isn't smooth tomorrow, you're gone!'

'Yes, staff!'

*

SELECTION

Candidates were only allowed to refer to instructors as 'staff'—even if you knew them personally. It was a psychological tactic, used to create distance. The instructors became nameless, faceless yelling machines—which made it easier for them to intimidate us mentally and physically.

I knew that shutting out this constant abuse was the only way I'd survive the week with my head intact. *Cut out the noise*, I kept thinking, not willing to let the instructors' barbs get in the way of my ambition.

After about an hour of standing at attention under the instructors' watchful eyes, we started to march around the parade ground doing some drill. Monotonous military discipline. This start to the course was different from what I remembered and I immediately regretted drinking so much water before arriving. Not more than twenty minutes had passed before the pressure in my bladder became unbearable.

'Excuse me, staff, can I go to the toilet?' I asked.

'No. Have some personal discipline,' he replied.

I did my best to put thoughts of waterfalls and raging rivers out of my mind but after another twenty minutes I was having full-blown stomach cramps.

'Excuse me, staff. Can I go to the toilet?' I asked again.

'I told you before: get some personal discipline!'

Almost bending over in pain at the pressure in my bladder, I considered the possibility of just going ahead and pissing my pants. After all, Alan Shepard, the first American into space, did it in his spacesuit on the launch pad, so why not me? I knew I'd be on the end of some horrendous verbal abuse but as I weighed up the alternatives I reckoned I could live with it. Just when I was at the point of no return, willing to be humiliated in front of a group of people I was trying to impress, another instructor spoke.

'Okay, you've got five minutes to get out of your uniforms and into some overalls. Go.'

His orders were like sweet music to my ears. I walked across the parade ground—well, it was more of a tiptoe, as each step needed careful consideration so not to pop my balloon. Seeing my salvation in the distance I wasn't going to wet my pants now—but as we moved toward our vehicles, the sweet music turned to a horrible cacophony when another instructor yelled at me, 'Run, you lazy prick!'

Although risking physical punishment for disobedience, I just couldn't do it, only able to shuffle toward the toilet block hunched over like an old man. Luckily, it wasn't too far away, but the thirty seconds or so it took to traverse the parade ground were probably the most painful I'd ever experienced and we were only in the first hour of the course!

This is going to be a long week, I thought as I let the liquid gush forth—that ecstatic moment making me forget everything else except how good it felt to piss.

Once we were in our overalls, the course really began, starting with a seemingly endless series of push-ups and sit-ups and an obstacle course that tested even the fittest of the candidates. We did all this wearing an M-17 gasmask—a still-functional though archaic piece of equipment designed and produced in the 1960s as a protection from chemical and biological agents. Forming a tight seal around the face, the masks reduced airflow to the wearer, causing accelerated fatigue, especially during physical exercise. They also made it hard to see and to communicate clearly, which was stressful and frustrating. As they were handed out I could see some of the other candidates exchanging confused glances but my face carried a look of resignation; I remembered all of this so vividly from my previous attempt at selection.

The last time I was here we'd had to complete an obstacle course that included an underground tunnel. The tunnel, a preformed concrete drainage pipe about 150 metres long and barely big enough to crawl in, ran about three metres under the base football field. When I'd entered the tunnel wearing the M-17, the enveloping darkness and closed surroundings, combined with the effects of the mask, made me shudder. I couldn't see my hand in front of my face, let alone the other end of the tunnel, and the rough cement on my skin was like a carpenter using sandpaper on a piece of wood. Struggling to breathe through the mask, I cringed at every scrape to my bare hands and knees, but my mood lifted when the light at the tunnel's end emerged out of the darkness. After twenty minutes in the tunnel I surfaced, elated to be standing upright again. The joy was short-lived, though. The entire obstacle course was to be repeated: another four times!

On the penultimate lap, the pain in my fingers was so sharp it felt like they'd been scraped down to the bone, so I used my knuckles instead. By the last lap, with the skin on my knees replaced by a blood-soaked patch on my overalls and my knuckles no longer recognisable, I resorted to lying on my side, kicking my legs and dragging my body forward using my elbows.

The experience left an indelible mark on my psyche.

Running towards the drain opening this time I hoped like hell that the practice of sending people through it was well and truly gone, although I had come prepared. Underneath my overalls I was wearing some knee pads just in case, a sneaky tactic that would no doubt result in physical punishment and/or emotional abuse if discovered, but with age and experience on my side I was willing to take that chance. The closer and closer we edged, the more vivid my memories became. I waited for one of the instructors to tell us to put our masks on and get in the tunnel. I could almost feel the pain in my knuckles but I allowed myself a wry smile knowing I had the knee pads. We came closer and closer to the tunnel's entrance and I began mentally preparing for the worst—and then we ran straight past the entrance!

I let out a sigh of relief but my euphoria was not to last long. The next hour or so involved full-on physical activity and by this time there were already a number of guys who had sought treatment for various injuries and ailments that would preclude them partaking any further in the course. I'd seen this the last time. A couple of guys probably had legitimate injuries and, although they wouldn't complete the course, they'd probably come back and have another crack. As for the rest of the 'injured', they were the guys who were unable or unwilling to subject themselves to further punishment, a convenient injury being the best way to withdraw while still maintaining your macho image and dignity.

Telling the difference between the legit guys and the ones who weren't was easy. I knew the look on the faces of the ones who were faking it because I'd considered doing the same thing, questioning why I was subjecting myself to this abuse and looking for the easy way out, but something, maybe pride or perhaps sheer stupidity, kept me in the game.

That's all it is, a game, I constantly reminded myself, even as the instructor who denied my toilet request stood over the top of me while I was in the middle of a push-up.

'You don't want to be here do you, Horsburgh?'

'Yes I do, staff.'

'Bullshit, I can tell you want to quit.'

'No, staff.'

Before coming back for my second attempt I had decided I'd use my own tactic of ignoring any abuse while in the middle of exercises. I'd learned that when I allowed the taunts to become personal it distracted me from completing the task I'd been given. So far, my tactic was working. As the day wore on, with an endless array of physical and mental punishments, I settled into a groove of almost mindless bliss (if pushing your body to its physical limits can be called 'bliss'), removing myself mentally and only being there in the physical body. I'd effectively taken my brain out and become a mechanical robot.

By late afternoon we gathered in a field next to the car park.

'See these tent bits here. That's your accommodation for the week. There are no instructions so you'll have to work it out between yourselves.'

The tent was a large marquee with a thousand pieces that we needed to put together if we wanted to sleep in any sort of comfort. Those of us who were still left at this time of the day worked together to erect our accommodation as the instructors stood back watching, waiting like vultures, ready to swoop down and devour the dead carcasses of those who failed. As we tried to figure out how to put the tent up we all caught sneaky glances of them writing notes about each candidate in their little black books. I had learned from my previous attempt at this course that everything was noted: comments by the candidates, observations, leadership qualities and so on. It would all be compared and assessed by a panel of selectors at the end of the course.

'Okay, it's now 11 pm. We're finished for the day. Get your uniforms ready for tomorrow and get some sleep,' an instructor said later that night.

Exhausted but excited that day one was over, I assessed my own health and saw that despite the torrid day of exercise I was in pretty good shape, even free of blistered feet, the enemy of many a candidate wearing boots during physical activity. A man could handle the verbal and psychological abuse if he trained his mind to it but once the blisters set in that was it: game over. After I showered, I prepped my uniform, spit polished my shoes and ironed my shirts for the inevitable inspection the next morning. After the instructor's observation about the smoothness of one of my companion's shirts I paid particular attention to mine but it was just as likely they would find something else to pick on.

With everything as smooth and as polished as I could get it I slumped into my bunk. I lay down and took a sneaky peek at my mobile phone, making sure it was on silent, and checked the time. The instructors may have been trying time torture on us but they'd obviously forgotten mobiles have clocks.

It was 1 am.

Hiding the phone again like a rebellious school kid, I rested my head on the pillow and was out like a light.

'Get out of bed, you maggots! You've got two minutes to be out on the parade ground.'

Snapping out of my sleep I opened my eyes to see one of the instructors standing at the entrance to the tent.

What time is it? I thought, groggily looking for my phone in the darkness. Despite my wearied state I was very careful to make sure the light from my phone didn't give it away because I knew I'd cop it if they found me using it.

It was 1.30 am.

'Hurry up!'

Within ninety seconds I was out on the parade ground with the other candidates, still half asleep and expecting the worst.

'You have a ten-kilometre pack march,' a particularly burly instructor said.

Short in stature, with a neck so broad it gave the impression that he didn't have one, this instructor had earned the nickname 'Ram Man', a throwback reference to one of the characters in the cartoon series *Masters of the Universe*. We'd secretly given each of the instructors humorous nicknames: Ram Man, Old Yella and Figjam were just some we had worked out during one of the very few and far between breaks. Figjam, an acronym for 'Fuck I'm Good Just Ask Me', was a particularly fitting moniker for a bloke who obviously enjoyed the power he had over us.

'You need to complete it within ninety minutes or you're out!' Ram Man added.

He pointed to some packs sitting on the ground, barely visible in the dull light.

'Grab a pack and put a cyalume stick on it. You leave in five minutes.'

Each of us hurriedly grabbed one of the packs, laden with about twenty-five kilograms of sand. Still half asleep I had, in my haste, chosen the pack with a broken strap. To make matters worse, these packs looked like they were straight from World War II. The strap was as skinny as a shoelace and now sported a large knot near the front of my shoulder to secure it. I put the pack on and gained a whole new appreciation for the soldiers of a bygone era, who not only had to carry such ordinary equipment but were under constant danger while they did so.

We took the cyalume sticks—waterproof plastic tubes that give off a luminous, usually green glow when you bend them sharply—and attached them to our packs so that the instructors could keep track of us. Then we began the march. Half jogging, half speed walking in the pitch-black night, I immediately regretted my decision to pull on a wet pair of boots in the rush to get dressed and make it to the parade ground on time.

As the kilometres clicked by, the increasing heat from an emerging blister and the chafing of the strategically placed knot on the front of my shoulder caused me to reduce my speed from a sluggish jog to a steady-paced walk. *Keep going*, I told myself over and over. I didn't have to come first in this trial—just complete it within the time frame. I put myself back into that robotic state of mind and just kept on, metre after metre, kilometre after kilometre ticking by. Before I knew it, the finish line was in sight. In the near distance I could see the guys who were either fitter than me or had better packs and no blisters keeling over and taking their packs off. If there had only been one guy, I'd have thought he was just buckling under the pressure, but a group of them meant the end.

'You've got ten minutes!' I heard the instructors shouting back to the men behind me. Seconds later I crossed the line. Bathed in a pool of sweat and reeling in pain I took the pack off my shoulders and attended to my blisters.

The ninety-minute deadline passed and those of us who had finished could see there were quite a few guys who were gone. They were immediately informed of the fact and the rest of us were ordered to shower and get back to our tent. While the thought of a shower thrilled me, I sensed sleep was out of the question. After showering,

I prepared for bed a second time, but dawn was already breaking and the instructors approached, signalling the start of another day.

The second day was much like the first: endless push-ups, miles of running and the all-too-familiar taunts from the instructing staff as we struggled to breathe in our gasmasks. Always on the go, we were not permitted to walk anywhere but had to run—except when we were told to leopard crawl, as was the case when we had to crawl from one end of a burr-infested football field to the other. During the day, Jack, one of the instructors who I knew prior to the course, came up to me on the parade ground while we were waiting for instruction on our next task.

'You think you're pretty shit hot, don't you, Horsburgh?'

'No, staff.'

'Yes you do. You think you're a better cricketer than Glenn McGrath.'

Shit!

It is amazing how little throwaway things you say and do come back to bite you on the arse. I closed my eyes and remembered, grudgingly, a conversation I'd had with Jack a few weeks before at the Police Academy bar in Goulburn.

After finishing high school in the small, predominantly farming community of Narromine in the mid-west of New South Wales, I'd taken a job at the local branch of the State Bank. One of my colleagues, a young, thinly framed guy named Glenn McGrath, had come to work at the bank about six months after I started, but Glenn and I already knew each other. We had been rivals in the small town's two main sporting pursuits: cricket and basketball.

Our sometimes bitter rivalry had begun a few years earlier, when we both played for the Backwater junior cricket team, of which I was the captain, holding sway over a number of other kids my age, including Glenn. I was the biggest, the loudest and the most dominant of the bunch, which I thought was a sure recipe for stardom. I'd bat at the top order, open the bowling and then, after a few overs, don the wicket keeping gloves for a stint behind the stumps, making sure when I paid my fifty cents to play on a Saturday morning I got my money's worth.

'Can I bowl?' Glenn would often ask.

'No. You're at fine leg!' I would say, giving him his marching orders to the boundary.

To be honest, I knew he could bowl a bit, but being so absorbed by my own desire for cricketing glory I chose to ignore it. For some reason, Glenn put up with being sent to the outer reaches of the outfield right up until it was time for us to graduate to the senior ranks. Not surprisingly, unable to show his skills to the senior cricketers because he was not given the opportunity to bowl, Glenn moved clubs to one where he'd be guaranteed to at least be able to contribute. For the next couple of seasons our rivalry intensified. Glenn's frustration was alleviated by a well-deserved barrage of short balls sent my way each time we played against his team.

During this time we also represented the open men's basketball team at country championships, carrying our extremely competitive natures to a new medium. Always singling each other out for special attention during training sessions, we never missed a chance to try to dominate each other, a situation we'd regularly recall as workmates at the bank.

'I used to hate you as a kid,' Glenn would inform me.

'I hated you too,' I'd retort.

'You never used to give me a bowl.'

'That's because you were shit.'

This tongue-in-cheek poke at each other provided much amusement, forming the basis of a friendship that lasted until Glenn's cricketing prowess was recognised by selectors from Sydney and he went on to become arguably the greatest fast bowler in the history of cricket. Glenn's achievements—and my reluctance to acknowledge them—became a source of ridicule and embarrassment for many years to come, a fact that Jack was now exploiting.

In his autobiography a few years later, Glenn described our cricketing days thus: 'There isn't really a great deal to write about my junior cricketing days except to say my skipper, a bloke named Shane Horsburgh, thought a broomstick had more ability than me!'

Back on the parade ground I spoke a little out of turn.

'I think he has proven that wasn't the case, staff,' I replied to Jack's taunts.

'Nice to see you're humble about it now. Not that you have much choice.'

Funnily enough he was right.

The banter between Jack and I led to laughter in the group and I was actually glad something so stupid had given us some slight relief from the constant barrage of physical and mental demands. I wasn't worried that the laughter was directed at me. After all, I'd caught up with and spoken to Glenn on many occasions after we left Narromine and all was forgiven . . . but it made for a good story.

11

Sleepless

At the end of the day the routine was very similar to that of the previous evening, and we finally got into bed at around 1.30 am. I could now fully understand the tactic of robbing us of our watches. Knowing the time had a calming effect. It meant we were better able to estimate how long an effort would be required, allowing us to conserve energy—a strategy that was not encouraged, as total commitment was expected at all times. Half expectedly, an instructor came into our tent just as the group had seemed to settle and sleep.

'Get up! Get up! You've got five minutes to be over in the lecture room.'

Taking another sneaky peek at my hidden phone I saw that it was now 2 am.

'Jesus, another half-hour sleep,' I said under my breath as I got dressed.

The groans from the twenty or so remaining candidates said it all. Although we were doing what was required, extreme exhaustion had begun to set in, a totally expected outcome welcomed by the directing staff, who wanted to see how each person coped with the stress.

Walking into the lecture room we sat down at individual desks to be addressed by Figjam.

'We are going to take a test. It will involve you listening closely and remembering what you hear.'

Figjam began reading a description of the terrorist hijacking of an Air France A300 Airbus in 1994, a memorable incident captured on television as members of the French Gendarmerie's GIGN counterterrorist team, the equivalent agency to the one I was attempting to join, stormed the aircraft while it was on the ground in Marseille, killing the hijackers and releasing the hostages. As Figjam read I recalled, even in my exhausted state, that I'd watched the dramatic incident unfold on TV a few years before. I listened intently, making a mental note of any details I thought we might be asked about: names, locations, persons killed and even the number of bullets fired. Retaining this sort of detail is difficult at any time, let alone when you are totally spent, but we did our best to take in every piece of information. After about ten minutes Figjam stopped and said, 'I'm going to ask you ten questions about what I just read. Your answers will be handed up and marked so get your pens ready.'

He read out the questions, but the effects of sleep deprivation were beginning to kick in. I was finding it increasingly difficult to concentrate and I was sure I was not alone. At the end of the exercise we handed our answers in and waited for further instruction.

'Okay. There are some weapons at the back of the room that you are going to assemble. When your name is called, go to one of the instructors. There are three weapons, so it doesn't matter where you go first—you have to do them all. Until your name is called, here are some puzzles to do.'

The whole thing was set up to make life as difficult as possible. The room was incredibly warm, rather cosy actually, and I was reaching that point where you struggle to keep your eyes open. My eyelids would slowly descend and I'd have to shake my head and snap them open again. To make matters worse, the lights were dimmed. I tried to complete the puzzles but my body was screaming for sleep. Constantly under the watchful eyes of the instructors, keen to note something of significance in their daily journals, it took everything I had not to close my eyes and drift into a restful slumber. I became almost delirious as I fought off the urge to take a quick power nap.

When it was my turn I went to the back of the room and sat down next to a weapon.

'This is an MP5 submachine pistol. Have you seen one of these?' the instructor asked.

'No, staff.'

'Good. Put it back together then.'

For the next fifteen minutes I studied each of the thirty or so pieces of this intricate little weapon, trying to determine which went where. A marvel of German engineering, the Heckler & Koch 9 mm MP5 had been the mainstay of tactical units and counterterrorist teams across the globe for the past thirty years. It was famously used by the British SAS during the resolution of the Prince's Gate siege at the Iranian Embassy in London in 1980. The weapon was a paradox—comfortable to hold, easy to use and able to be fired accurately by just about anybody. At the same time it was delicate, intricate and complicated in its make-up with a multitude of moving parts, including a locking roller mechanism that allowed the projectile to leave the barrel before any of the internal workings moved, which negated any recoil. As the MP5 took shape and its parts appeared to be in place, the instructor, who we hadn't yet given a nickname, said, 'Have you finished?'

'Yes, staff . . . all except for this bit,' I said, holding up a tiny spring. Try as I might, I couldn't figure out its purpose and fit.

He heartily laughed, demonstrating the first bit of humour I'd seen from the staff since the course had started.

'That's a firing pin spring.'

'Ah, okay then . . .' I said, allowing myself a little laugh.

'Wouldn't have been able to do much without it, but overall it was a pretty good effort for a first-timer.'

'Thanks, staff.'

After completing the other weapons it was back to my seat—to tackle some more puzzles and resume the battle with my eyelids. A couple of hours later the last of our group completed the exercise. As we walked back to the tent I saw the first rays of sunlight coming over the horizon and knew it would only be a matter of minutes before we were roused from our sleep. I lay down in my bunk anyway, fully clothed and with my boots still on, and fell asleep in seconds. About fifteen minutes later the screech of a police siren outside the tent jolted me from my slumber. It was our wake-up call. Reluctantly I rose from my bunk, hurriedly ate some breakfast and made sure I had everything I needed for a new day of torment.

Around mid-morning, after we completed the obligatory push-ups (a popular armed forces bastardisation method) we were driven to the base pool complex for a physical training session. I was relieved at first to be doing a different activity, but I soon changed my tune. The PT session involved constant sprints across the pool and an endless series of torturous 'tea bags' (jumping in the deep end, touching the bottom and getting out again). Using muscles that didn't often get a work-out caused a build-up of lactic acid in my system and as nausea grew I ran to the grassed area around the pool and violently vomited.

'I hope you're going to clean that up?' Ram Man quipped.

'Yes, staff,' I said, wiping the remnants of my breakfast from the side of my mouth.

Toward the end of the session I saw the instructors standing around in a group having a laugh about something. It didn't take long to find out why.

'Everyone line up at the three-metre diving board,' Figjam ordered. After we were lined up he added with smirk, 'Everybody has to do a somersault off the diving board before we leave here.'

It was yet another method of taking us out of our comfort zone but one which provided much amusement for the instructors as they watched our feeble attempts to complete the task. Fortunately, when I was growing up in Narromine, our local pool had a three-metre diving board. I had spent many long summers doing somersaults with my mates and although I was no expert I could at least do one without hurting myself. Some of the other guys weren't so lucky but it didn't seem to matter. The pain of hitting the water with your back or your head was minor compared to what we had already been through, so everyone completed the task to the best of their ability, even if some of the efforts were so bad we couldn't help but to burst into laughter.

Thankful to see the end of the session, we were sitting on the bus waiting for the next bout of torture when the psychologist who had been watching our sessions poked her head in the door and asked to see one of the candidates outside. She went everywhere with us, always observing, always taking notes on how the torture we were enduring was affecting our mental state.

'You're all nuts!' I heard her say jokingly one day, obviously recognising a certain amount of masochism was required to sign up for this abuse.

We watched her talk to our course mate and it was obvious from his body language that she was recommending he did not continue. When they'd finished speaking he was whisked away by the staff. Our numbers had dwindled down to sixteen but in some ways I envied him because he was now free to go home and get away from the pain. This thought became even stronger and more profound when the instructors boarded the bus.

'He's been removed because the psych assessed that he wouldn't cut it, especially for what we have in store for you this afternoon.'

The bus was silent.

Fuck, I thought. *They've just put us through the wringer, what else could they possibly do?*

The afternoon exercise was one straight out of the sadist's handbook. Splitting into teams of eight we were given an imaginary 'mission': transporting an injured man and some vital equipment back to the safety of our base before the other team. The 'man' was a sand-filled dummy weighing eighty kilograms and the 'vital equipment' consisted of a large tractor tyre and some ammunition boxes with rope handles, as well as our twenty-five kilogram sand-filled packs with shoelace straps.

We set off on the mission not knowing how far we had to go or how long the exercise would take but we knew from the start that to complete the task successfully we'd need teamwork, and a regular routine that would let us share the load. Our pattern was simple: count for thirty steps, put everything down, rotate around the stretcher to a different position to distribute the pain, pick the load up again and continue on until the next rotation—a monotonous cycle that lasted several hours. Every so often an instructor would bark an order: 'Gas! Gas! Gas!' That was the cue for us to put our M-17s on.

As if trudging through the exercise unable to breathe properly wasn't enough, another instructor would pipe up at different intervals to make the shitty experience of carrying the stretcher even more unpleasant.

'Put everything down. Everyone sit down on the ground with crossed legs and your hands on your head.'

This is new, I thought, but there was no way I could comprehend what we were in for. The simple act of sitting cross-legged on the ground with your hands on your head, a gasmask on your face and a twenty-five kilogram pack on your back was extremely painful. Putting somebody in a 'stress position' like this for long periods of time is often used as an interrogation technique, and it was working to great effect.

During the carry, I watched a member of the other team collapse with exhaustion. We later found out he'd been transported to hospital for extreme dehydration, which had caused the early symptoms of muscle meltdown, a potentially fatal condition brought on by over-exertion. The overheated muscle accumulates calcium, causing a chemical reaction which is harmful to the kidneys. I knew it was dangerous because a guy doing a similar course about ten years earlier at the Police Academy in Goulburn had died during a long run on a hot day, simply because his body had run out of water. I didn't know what the wash-up from the coronial enquiry into his death was, but we had been ordered to take regular drinks to prevent an incident like that happening again. Some guys had obviously not listened. Unfortunately, any thoughts of others were a secondary consideration as the struggle to place one foot after the next became my primary concern.

After a few hours, Figjam approached a member of my team and said, 'Do you want a Mars bar?'

Thinking that Figjam was just looking after his welfare, he took the chocolate and ate it.

'You jack prick!' Figjam screamed. 'What about your mates?'

Once again, the strategy of testing people when they were tired and vulnerable had found another victim. Taking the chocolate for himself instead of sharing it with his mates would see him labelled as weak and selfish; a failure of character that would surely go into Figjam's black book. I was becoming increasingly aware of the tactic, blocking out the taunting and abuse to concentrate more easily on what I was doing.

Toward the end of the mission, well into the darkness by this time, another instructor yelled at us as he pointed to a bus parked on the side of the road about 400 metres in front of us: 'When you get to the bus it's all finished!'

Knowing that we had only 400 metres to go before this pain and torture would all be over gave us a boost and our pace quickened—but as we neared the bus its motor roared and it drove another kilometre down the road.

'You were too late! You'd better catch it!' another instructor screamed.

Keeping to our previous pace and rhythm we once again chased the bus. Something strange came over me. I realised the weight of the dodgy pack on my back with the thin straps didn't hurt anymore—in fact, I felt no pain. I was completely absorbed in the tempo of our footsteps. We approached the bus. The bastards drove it off again! They were dangling a carrot in front of a horse.

When it happened a third time I thought, *Okay, fuckwits, enough is enough!*

They must have had mental telepathy. The bus stopped and we were allowed to stow the equipment. As we packed up our gear I could sense a begrudging respect coming from most of the instructors, who were happy with the effort put in by both teams.

'That only took you about five hours,' one of them said to us.

'How far did we go?' one of the other candidates asked.

'About twelve k.'

By proving we could tough out even the most sadistic shit they could throw at us, we had earned their respect. Having reduced the original group by half, I think they also felt that unless someone picked up a serious injury which prevented them from completing the course, those who were left had a real chance of joining the unit. This feeling was confirmed later that evening when we were permitted to sleep for a full six hours, our first real rest in three days. Although the next few days were still extremely physical affairs, the instructors toned it down a bit. They knew it was entirely possible we'd be working together in the near future.

On the last day the successful candidates would be told whether they'd be invited to join Tactical Operations and begin CT training for the upcoming Sydney Olympics. I was fairly confident I'd done enough to be selected but then I remembered I'd felt the same six years earlier. One by one we were escorted into an interview room where every detail of our lives for the past week was regurgitated in full. Every missed push-up, every sideways look, every failure and triumph was noted. I have no doubt they had already made their decision based on this information, but it was like riding an emotional roller-coaster as I listened to the debrief and looked for as many positive clues as I could to work out if I was successful. Finally the moment came. After a few little whispers between them and with me leaning forward in my chair, anxiously looking on, it was Figjam who uttered the words: 'We are going to extend you an invitation.'

The disappointment of six years earlier instantly dissolved. The months of running through the bush with a pack on my back had paid off, but instead of elation I just felt relieved it was all over. Milling around the car park, those who had already learned their fate waited for the results of everybody else's interviews. In the few seconds after they had left the room and begun walking over to us I could tell from their body language how they went. Looks of relief, a long stride and the odd fist pump indicated success, while slumping shoulders, a slow pace and a look of disappointment told me the opposite. As I had been in the latter group before and experienced the shattering the news of failure, I felt really sorry for them. One hundred and fifty officers initially applied to do the course, whittled down to thirty who'd actually started and now only fifteen were left to face the music. Of these, ten were deemed to be suitable and I was very glad I was one of them. After commiserating with the guys who missed out and congratulating the ones who would be joining me, I got in my car and drove out of the gates of hell. Too tired to celebrate I just went straight home.

As I came in the door my wife, Nicole, looked at me in amazement, as if some strange man had just walked in. With grazed skin on just about every exposed area of my body, my features gaunt after having lost six kilograms during the week, I was a shadow of the man who'd left our home a mere seven days earlier.

'Jesus. What happened to you?' she said incredulously.

I recounted some of the week's events as she filled a bath so I could soak and relax. I poured a good amount of disinfectant into the water and climbed in. Within seconds I jumped out screaming.

'My balls are burning!'

'I put some Dettol in for your grazes!'

'Shit! So did I!'

Even though my whole body was on fire we both had a good laugh. It was a pleasantly humorous end to what had been a very serious week.

I'm not sure if it was being home with my wife or the hilarity of my balls being on fire but whatever it was all the built-up tension completely dissipated and I eagerly anticipated starting my new job.

12

'You'll Need a Thick Skin!'

In February 2000, I received confirmation I was to be transferred to the Tactical Operations Unit to begin the build-up training for the Olympics. I was excited beyond belief and looking forward to completing my specialist training courses over the next six months to qualify for the role. However, as is so often the case, one part of my life was coming up roses while another was gradually starting to crumble. My relationship with Nicole had begun to develop major cracks. We'd recently moved to a house in Sydney's north-western suburb of Baulkham Hills that required a major overhaul, so, in between long days of training, I was trying to renovate a large five-bedroom house. Oblivious to the developing rift in my relationship, I concentrated on my career—my method of dealing with emotional problems.

I was, I thought, on top of the world. I had qualified for a job which, in my eyes, was the epitome of what it meant to be a real man—the ultimate adrenaline-fuelled ego trip which served to reaffirm my rapidly inflating view of my own importance. I was now at the beginning of a journey into an elite world where being macho was the norm and weakness was not tolerated. Issues such as emotional and physical intimacy were secondary to maintaining the illusion of a tough exterior—but this was beginning to take its toll on Nicole.

I met Nicole when a friend introduced us at the NSW Police Academy in Goulburn in 1989. She was a tall, leggy blond and I was captivated by her smile. We hit it off immediately. We were inseparable and spent as much time with each other between policing lessons as we possibly could. After we both graduated and moved to our respective suburban stations in Sydney, our relationship continued to blossom. We became engaged after eighteen months and then married a year later. A house, two children and the clichéd family dog soon followed, but after eight years of marriage the honeymoon had soured.

'Why do you have to do this job?' she had asked before the transfer came through.

'Because it's what I want to do.'

'What about us?'

'What do you mean us? I'm doing this for *you*.'

Horse, my nickname, was proving more apt than I knew. I was running a race, believing I was leading by a furlong and would be able to claim the ultimate prize once I'd crossed the finish line—but I had my blinkers on.

I just didn't get it. In chasing my macho dream I actually believed everything I was doing was for the good of the family.

'Bullshit,' Nicole snapped. 'It's for *you*. It's always been about *you*. The same thing happened with the dog squad years ago.'

At some level I knew she was right but I wasn't willing to accept it. In 1994 I had left her and our six-month-old son, Alex, to go back to the academy in Goulburn to do a five-month-long dog handlers' course. Still suffering from a bout of postnatal depression, Nicole found my absence during the week particularly hard as she struggled to cope with a young baby. I was aware of the angst I'd caused but her concerns fell on deaf ears because of my single-minded focus on what I wanted to achieve in the near future.

Now, blinkers still firmly in place, I was leaving her on her own again.

Back at my new workplace the courses we were doing were very diverse. The special weapons and tactics course was the most intense but also the most thrilling—we were taught how to use specialist weapons such as the MP5 with deadly precision and the tactics involved in building assaults. The course was run in the same vein as the original selection course, with the instructors doing their best to belittle and humiliate us. I'd heard a rumour that on a previous SWAT course one of the instructors had actually urinated on the back of one of the students while he was doing a firearms drill. As someone who had previously instructed police in firearms tactics I saw this sort of deliberate intimidation as a little archaic, an outdated method of teaching that did not augur well for working relationships after the course.

I understood that they wanted to test our physical toughness, but this was a bit over the top. It certainly didn't create the sense of comradeship that you'd be relying on when push came to shove. Given that we would need as much time as possible to become proficient in each of the disciplines, I also thought that concentrating on the skills to be learned instead of bullying them into the students would be a much more practical use of our time. Thankfully, as the course wore on and the instructing staff recognised that those who remained would make the grade, the policy of bastardisation slowed down, but it was never going to make up for the resentment that had already built within our group.

During air operations training, a CT course centring on resolving hijackings, an incident occurred that reminded me of something a mate from my home town of Narromine told me before I even joined the cops: 'If you can get through the cops without becoming a hypocrite, then you've done well.'

Pete was a police officer himself, so his words had struck a chord with me. Since then I'd witnessed many police who, as they progressed through the ranks, suddenly rallied against behaviour or mannerisms they had once displayed themselves—primarily out of concern for their own jobs. They adopted the 'do as I say, not as I do' approach to leadership, a sure-fire method of alienating those under their charge.

During the Air Ops course we had to resolve an imaginary hijacking incident on a commercial jet aircraft. The aircraft, an expensive mock-up of a Boeing 747, was an exact replica (albeit made of wood), with the dimensions and structure of the actual plane. Our task was to stealthily approach the aircraft, use ladders to climb onto the wings and resolve the incident by assaulting the cabin through the exit doors over the wings. Armed with specially adapted MP5s that fired rounds of simmunition (a type of paintball that could be chambered and fired from a real weapon), we approached the aircraft with ladders in hand. Rapidly edging nearer and nearer, we heard a shot from inside the cabin followed by a loud 'Oh, fuck!'

It was obvious what had happened. An instructor had been standing on the wing to video the assault, so that we could watch it after the exercise had concluded, during the debrief. He had opened the door to capture footage of us as we came in and had been shot by one of the 'terrorists', who had mistaken him for us. We had a bit of a giggle that one of the instructional staff had been shot but we totally understood how it could have happened and kept on with the exercise until it was completed. Our senior instructor, one of the best teachers I'd seen but riddled with demons of his own, was angry that we'd seen his team stuff things up. When rumours began to circulate that one of the staff had had an 'unintentional discharge' or UD, the cover-ups began. Firing a weapon when you don't mean to is probably the most embarrassing thing a tactical operator can do, as it challenges the carefully constructed image of capability and competency you work so hard to project. In that sense it is really no different to the stigma surrounding premature ejaculation!

I'd been involved in firearms instruction for a long time and had seen many UDs of varying degrees. I'd even had one on the practice range myself when I fired at a paper target before the instructor had given the order. From my perspective, the instructor's so-called mistake was merely a nervous reaction to the oncoming assault, totally understandable seeing that twelve guys armed with submachine guns were about to riddle him with paint bullets (that incidentally hurt like hell when they hit). Unfortunately, the instructors didn't see it that way and quickly went into damage control to ensure their image wasn't tarnished. They called a briefing to discuss the matter and the 'how to treat people like children' playbook soon came out. They failed to take our many years of shared police and military experience into account.

'Okay,' said the senior instructor. 'Nothing happened. There were no shots fired before you got to the aircraft.'

I looked around at the other guys in my assault team and could see they felt the same frustration I did.

Is this the best excuse you've got? Denial! I thought. Davo, an experienced police officer who had been in the Tactical Operations Unit a few years earlier and was now rejoining for the Olympic program, didn't hold back.

'It doesn't matter *why* it happened, we don't give a shit, but we heard a shot so don't treat us like kids. It's no big deal.'

The senior instructor was infuriated at the perceived challenge to his authority and his face turned as red as a radish. Veins started to bulge along the length of his forehead and he looked like he was ready to explode.

'It is a big deal! The rumour is that it was a UD and I won't have those rumours circulating about my staff!'

Worried about how the staff was perceived, the instructors had made a mountain out of a molehill instead of admitting a mistake had been made. If they had just admitted it, I have no doubt we would all have got over it and moved on.

At the completion of my courses I was now a fully qualified operator. I received the full gamut of standard issue tactical equipment: the menacing dark overalls, thick body armour, thigh holsters, Bollé goggles, knee pads and Kevlar helmet, along with SF-9 stun grenades, radios, spare ammunition and wound dressings, which were secured in a vest worn over the body armour itself. We were literally dressed to kill. Our 'kit', as we called it, weighed around twenty-five kilograms, giving an air of authority and invincibility that made it easy to intimidate offenders—one of the most effective ways to make them submit. This approach was also used to great effect on some of us newbies.

Iliya, a veteran with over fifteen years' field experience, was one of the great characters in my new workplace and one of the best shit-stirrers I'd ever met. Looking like a mix between Mr Bean and Jerry Seinfeld, Iliya's resemblance to these characters almost guaranteed he would weave his own brand of hilarity into any situation, even when he was taking the piss out of everybody, including our bosses. Seen by the hierarchy as a troublemaker, due to his fondness for speaking out against the establishment, Iliya always said what he had to say with a wicked sense of humour.

As luck would have it, Iliya would be the team leader on my first operational job. Assembling in the car park underneath the Sydney Police Centre, we gathered the necessary equipment while he gave us a run-down on the operational procedures. According to Iliya the job itself was nothing special—a routine drug warrant. We were going along only because the offenders were allegedly in possession of firearms. Because it was my first job I was a little nervous and I wanted to make sure I didn't muck anything up.

'You're driving the ERV, Horse,' Iliya said.

'Okay,' I said, my nerves calming down a little.

I considered myself a pretty good driver and figured driving the ERV minimised my chances of making a mistake. The Emergency Response Vehicle was a modified Chevy Suburban, a large American 4WD adapted to fit the huge amount of equipment that we might need at a moment's notice. Looming very large when driven on the street, the hulking black ERV was a beast to behold. We pulled out of the car park and I remember thinking that, even for a large vehicle, its handling seemed a bit sluggish. Almost immediately I noticed a flashing warning light on the dash and in a subtle 'look over there' manoeuvre I pointed to something outside the ERV to redirect everyone's attention and discreetly disengaged the brake.

Or so I thought.

Iliya, sitting in the front passenger seat, looked at me with a childish grin on his face. Smiling nervously at him I looked in the rear-vision mirror to see if our two other companions had seen what happened. Thankfully they hadn't.

'Don't worry. I won't tell anyone,' he said.

I laughed, knowing his silence was too much to ask for—I knew the typical operator sense of humour too well. To his credit, he didn't say anything . . . until we arrived at the command post and a proper audience was present. Standing near the rear of the vehicle for an impromptu briefing, Iliya couldn't resist.

'You know Horse drove halfway here with the handbrake on?' he said.

They all had a bit of a laugh and although my face was a little red and I was slightly embarrassed I refocused on the job at hand and started getting my body armour, over vest and helmet on as I grabbed an MP5 from the gun rack.

'You're with me,' Iliya said as I finished putting my kit on.

Even though he'd just embarrassed me in front of the others, I was glad to be with him. After gearing up we walked down the quiet inner-western suburban street toward the target premises. Well-established trees along the length of the boulevard provided oodles of shade for the hundreds of cars whose drivers had been lucky enough to get a space in this densely populated area.

It was very quiet, meaning we needed to be too.

With one eye on the target premises and another on the ground in front of me, I moved forward. Our approach was as stealthy as any I'd done in training.

'When we get into position can you cover the windows down the side of the house?' Iliya asked as we drew closer.

'No sweat.'

Reaching our position at the front right side of the house, I raised my MP5 from the slung position and aimed it toward the windows so I could provide cover to the team as they entered the premises but also to ensure no one inside could use the windows as an escape route.

Everything was deathly quiet as I watched and waited for the team to begin their assault then . . . in the soundless surrounds . . . the noise of metal striking cement rang out like a church bell. I looked down as the twenty-nine round magazine that was supposed to be attached to the base of the MP5 fell in slow motion and rattled at my feet.

Oh, fuck! I thought as I bent down to pick it up, hoping no one else had heard the clatter.

'You're not having a good day, are you?' Iliya said. 'Don't worry, I won't tell anyone.'

'Yeah, right! I've heard that one before!'

'Don't beat yourself up. I've done it myself. The magazine catch can sometimes get caught on the over vest.'

'Nice to know . . . now.'

Luckily for me, in the brief moments following my embarrassing mistake the entry team's attention was concentrated on more pressing matters. Five guys clad in black stood in single file on one side facing the front door while another, commonly referred to as the 'hammer man', stood on the other. Wielding a 'universal key' guaranteed to open just about any lock, he made light work of the standard-looking front door with the fifteen-kilogram sledgehammer.

'Police! Police! Police!' they yelled as one by one they disappeared inside.

For the next few minutes the standard room entry communication calls of 'With you!', 'With me!' and 'Clear!' could easily be heard from our position in the street, filling me with excitement. I knew in time I'd be doing entries as well.

And it did help me to briefly forget my mistake.

Within a few minutes the team of six operators emerged from the premises shooting Iliya a 'nothing here' look.

'Horsey, I've been on hundreds of jobs and most of them turn out like this. The intelligence is either crap or over-exaggerated,' Iliya said.

'How many do you reckon are fair dinkum?'

'About ten per cent.'

While my first trip out was rather uneventful it was still a steep learning curve. I'd need to adapt quickly, learning not just the tricks of the trade but also the fine art of sledging.

'Just remember one thing,' Iliya added once the job was done. 'When you come to this place you get issued with three things: body armour, a submachine gun and a thick skin.'

'Okay, I'll remember.'

'And you'll need the thick skin the most . . . trust me.'

13

From the Attic to the Basement

The excitement of the upcoming Olympics was beginning to reach its peak. Inside I was abuzz, just like the city as a whole. My home situation, however, had gone from bad to worse to atrocious. Due to our ever-increasing training schedule I was spending more and more time away, too caught up in my own ego trip to think about what was really important. I was on the brink of achieving everything I'd hoped for. I was part of the biggest security detail for the biggest sporting event in the world and I had to prove I was part of the team and, most importantly, that I was one of the boys.

About a week out from the big show, Nicole asked if we could talk in the bedroom.

'I want to split up,' she said as we sat down together on the bed.

Shocked, but not really surprised, I put my head in my hands and began to weep. Funny really. I'd spent years creating this image and countless hours convincing myself, and others, of how hard I was, yet when my wife told me she wanted to leave the whole macho facade came crashing down in an instant.

'Why?' I naively asked.

'You're never here for us. All you care about is your fucking job.'

She was remarkably calm. When I took my head from my hands and looked at her she had an almost pitying expression on her face, one that said I should have seen this coming.

'Even when you're home you only talk about what's going on in your world. You're here, but not really.'

I couldn't speak. I knew deep down inside that what she was saying was true, but I was also feeling a bit self-righteous: what I'd done *was* for the family's sake.

'Where will I go?' I asked.

It was a desperate plea for mercy. I was hoping she would feel enough pity for me to delay the separation and give me another chance. I felt vulnerable, and I was resorting to emotional games, trying to make her feel sorry for me, but I was clutching at straws.

'I've thought about it. You can stay at my mum's.'

She already had it all worked out. Her frustration had obviously been stewing and simmering for some time. She'd reached boiling point and finally decided enough was enough. As bad as our relationship had become, I would have continued on regardless—like other unhappily married men—but Nicole had clearly decided that she couldn't go on any longer.

We didn't speak, we just embraced. We lay on the bed crying in each other's arms. Our shared family dreams were coming to an end.

Not surprisingly, the incidence of relationship breakdowns in my line of work was very high. More than half the guys I worked with were divorced. Long, committed work hours and overactive egos had been the death knell for their relationships. I had thought I was immune, too wrapped up in the 'that will never happen to me' mindset.

The other guys probably did too.

The next day I moved into the basement of my mother-in-law's house, a short distance from my place. While I was on good terms with Joan and was very grateful for her kindness in allowing me to stay, I still felt deeply embarrassed. But there was no alternative. The four-man CT teams we had been split into months before the Olympics were dictated by where we lived in Sydney and every team was allocated a 4WD to be used each day to transport us to and from our stand-by venue near the main athletics stadium. A move out of the area would be too difficult for my team to manage so I would have to suck it up.

The first night at Joan's was a long, lonely, sleepless affair. As I lay on a mattress on the tiled floor of the basement a thousand thoughts ran through my head. *Is this really happening? Are my children going to be okay? Can I fix this? How dare she do this to me? What are my mates going to think when they find out I'm staying at my mother-in-law's?* At times throughout the night I wept uncontrollably, a deep sadness filling me every time I thought about my children, my wife and what my life had become. At other times I shook with anger at the thought of having everything I loved being taken away from me, determined to fight hard to keep them because I thought that's what a man does. Eventually, mentally and emotionally exhausted, I fell asleep.

In the morning the most pressing concern I had was how I was going to explain my new living arrangements to the boys in my team. Luckily I had become very good mates with Stewie and Sean, two of the guys I had done my selection and training courses with. I thought they would understand my predicament but even so, I prepared myself for the good natured piss-taking I would undoubtedly receive from them. Not willing to let strong emotions or sledging from workmates get in the way of my job, I threw myself into the Olympic whirl, trying to put the events of the past few days behind me.

Once the games started I was working six twelve-hour days a week, with no time to dwell on what might have been—especially given there were so many good-looking girls from every corner of the globe frequenting Sydney's hottest nightspots to take my mind off things and help me forget any lingering feelings of inadequacy. The 'sports carnival' as we called it, a throwback to school athletics meets, was party central.

I'd heard many people wanted to escape Sydney when the carnival was on, not comfortable with the crowds flocking to the harbour city, but I had a totally different experience. As CT operators we were given special passes allowing us unlimited access anywhere we wished to go. Called the 'Infinity Pass', it authorised us to attend any sporting event in plain clothes, supposedly to observe the crowds but in reality to watch the spectacular unfold. Undoubtedly the highlight was when Stewie, Sean and I sat with the Australian swimming team in the athlete's seating area to watch Cathy Freeman win gold in the 400 metres. The atmosphere was electric. Near the finish line we could clearly see the relief on Cathy's face, the weight of the nation's expectation lifted off her shoulders as the crowd went nuts. We were there in our shorts, T-shirts and running shoes, jumping up and down and cheering along with everyone else. Supplying a counterterrorist capability for the Olympics had become a secondary consideration to having a good time—and if we weren't watching the spectacle, we were heading out for a few drinks whenever we had time off.

With my male pride still in tatters I was seeking the short-term affections of any unsuspecting traveller to try to cover up the immense pain I still felt (but refused to show) after my marriage break-up. Our favourite haunt was the Heineken Bar at Darling Harbour, a two-storey temporary venue reserved for the exclusive entertainment of Dutch athletes and friends, holders of a Netherlands passport and . . . the police. All we had to do was flash the 'Bluey'—our affectionate name for the standard police ID—and we were in. It was a great place to have a few drinks, dance to a bit of traditional Dutch oompah music and flirt with girls.

When the excitement of the Olympics was over, day-to-day life at the unit returned to a more normal structure. Emergency equipment was checked at the start of every shift, followed by a weights and/or physical training session. Our training regimens were only interrupted by the odd high-risk job. The repetitive, routine nature of the work meant that I didn't really notice time passing by. Weeks became months, and before I knew it I had been in the unit for over a year. All the while I was honing my sledging skills—a common way to pass the time. It was a game, putting the other guys down—a constant to-and-fro as each guy tried to prove who the biggest man was.

One night, about a year after the Olympics, I was rostered on a night shift. As I roamed around, bored, I noticed that Eric, one of the operators who joined the unit at the same time I did, had left his intra-office email account open. Thinking I was being particularly funny, I pretended I was him and wrote a witty (or so I thought) email explaining why I (Eric) was unhappy at the unit, pleading with the other operators to stop picking on me, otherwise I would leave. I then sent the email to all fifty or so of the other operators. It backfired in a big way when Eric approached the boss to seek a transfer. Apparently I'd been closer to the truth than I imagined.

Fortunately, I was able to apologise before he followed through with the transfer but there were other examples of bullying that didn't end so well. Another operator, a slightly overweight but highly experienced character who did not fit the SWAT team stereotype, was a popular target for ridicule in the unit. I'd heard many remarks aimed at him—'you've got a fat arse', 'you're hopeless' or 'you're not worthy of working here'—comments that were often delivered in a joking manner but were really meant seriously. Not surprisingly I heard that the anger and resentment at being the butt of people's jokes came to a head during the early hours of a twelve-hour night shift, when the operator in question reached his tipping point. Turning to face his tormentors, a core group of guys, most of whom thought they were Figjams in their own right, he drew his police-issue .40-calibre Glock pistol, pointed it at them and yelled, 'Shut the fuck up!'

Not surprisingly, the guys backed down, but even as the dust from this incident was settling a change of behaviour was not apparent. The taunting and bullying were systemic, part of the organisational culture, much like the dynamic between groups of boys in a schoolyard, and so could not be suppressed.

I am not entirely blameless. I too participated in this game, not yet able to understand what effect it had on others and too caught up in hiding my own insecurities to really care. In the early years of my career in special operations, I was firmly entrenched in a militaristic, conformist culture, but my personal feelings of discomfort and frustration began to grow. The result was a discontent that bordered on apathy.

14

Dead Man's Trigger

There was a bit of a shake-up in October 2001—a welcome change to the pace of our normal routine. In the preceding months a rotation of three-man sniper teams had been deployed on a week-on, week-off basis to a sleepy country town in the north-west of New South Wales to observe a bloke who had become a cause for concern for the townsfolk and the local police.

The Tactical Operations Unit had two main divisions—the sniper stream and the assaulter stream—and there was a healthy rivalry between them. As a part of the assaulter stream I'd never had any interest in becoming a sniper, preferring to remain close to the action. Kicking in the door of a house before searching for and arresting dangerous offenders was my idea of tactical policing, but the snipers saw things differently. They were highly skilled, and had to complete a long, difficult course before qualifying as marksmen. Trained to use the Remington 700 sniper rifle in both urban and rural environments, they were most often called upon to provide protection for the assault teams. Referring to us as knuckle draggers, the sniper stream believed they were a precision instrument, a belief reflected in their unofficial motto: 'One shot. One kill.'

Wankers!

From our perspective, the snipers' only chance of injury was the possibility of getting a piece of coconut from an Iced VoVo blown into their eyes as they watched us do the hard yards through the iris of a high-powered scope.

In reality we all worked together as a team but the good-natured banter was entertaining nonetheless.

The reason for the snipers' deployment was an elderly gentleman who lived on a farm about ten kilometres outside of town had made an unusual fashion choice: wearing a fully operational body bomb strapped to his chest underneath his overalls everywhere he went—even when he came into town to do his shopping! Having very little information about the suspect, our sniper teams set up an observation post (OP) on the hillside overlooking his property to keep a keen eye on his movements. Months passed and we gathered a mountain of intelligence on him so we could make a plan to capture him safely. Unfortunately it wasn't going to be easy.

Information had come to light: if he was approached by police or anybody who looked like police he would detonate the device by way of a concealed dead man's trigger. The device itself, a large homemade pipe bomb, scored on the outside with diagonal lines to increase shrapnel damage, was connected to the dead man's trigger in his pocket via a rudimentary wiring system. It was a simple enough mechanism. All he had to do was depress the trigger and then flick a small switch to arm the device. Once he lifted his finger from the trigger, the bomb would detonate. This simple yet ruthlessly efficient system certainly ruled out walking up to him and saying, 'You're nicked, mate.' Apart from wearing the homemade bomb everywhere he went, he also had an inclination for stalking around his rural property, paranoid that the police—or even worse, the Indonesians—were coming to get him. After several weeks, it all seemed fairly routine for the snipers, who'd been observing his antics 24/7, watching him check and then double-check his sheds for security, pointing his rifle at high-flying jets so he could see them in his telescopic sights, and caring for his small dog like it was his child.

All in all, we weren't exactly sure how we were going to get him. Fate, however, stepped in to lend us a helping hand.

There was a dirt road adjacent to his property, normally a rarely travelled byway. One day an antique Model T Ford was cruising down the road at a lively thirty kilometres an hour. Its occupants were participating in a vintage car rally, meandering through the forests of the region on a lovely spring day. Taking in the countryside around him, the driver of the Ford did not see the little white Maltese terrier run into the middle of the road until it was too late. Standing at his letterbox near the road, rifle in hand, the old man had seen it all, and now he stormed toward the car brandishing his weapon in the air. Startled not only by hitting the dog but also by the response from the dog's owner, the driver of the Model T cranked up the engine and took off—a totally understandable response.

Picking up the lifeless carcass of his beloved pet, the old man walked back onto his property and disappeared into his dwelling. A few minutes later the snipers reported that he'd gotten onto a motorised bicycle and was heading in the direction of town. The homemade bicycle was engineered from parts he had collected. In addition to the bike, we'd heard he'd also built his own working helicopter and machine tooled his own pistols, which worked just like bought ones. For this alone, he deserved our begrudging respect. He was the epitome of the mad professor—a brilliant mind that had developed an unhealthy level of paranoia.

When he reached town he walked into the local police station to report the incident with the Model T and from the prominent bulge in the chest area of his overalls it was obvious to the officer on duty that he was packing more than an unhappy disposition. Standing with his hand firmly placed in his pocket, no doubt with his finger on the dead man's trigger, he demanded the police give him the details of the vehicle's owner—not because he wanted to exchange details but to exact his revenge. The officer at the desk, a local sergeant who had full knowledge of what was going on and the level of our unit's involvement, was cool and calm as he spoke to him, organising for him to come back in a few days so that the police could take a statement and give him the other party's particulars, an agreement that seemed to appease his anger.

Back in Sydney, one of our senior sergeants, a cool, articulate supervisor named Colin, had made cautious progress on a suitable plan for the old man's arrest—a plan that would see both the mad professor and everybody else involved in the operation come through safely. I liked Colin. Not only was he an extremely competent leader, making good timely decisions when they needed to be made instead of just trying to look after his own arse, but he also took a genuine interest in the welfare of the blokes under his charge. In the months prior to what became known as 'Dog Day', Colin had meticulously researched any possible way to arrest this guy without harm. In his thorough preparation for the inevitable moment he had contacted a number of other agencies, including the Special Air Service (SAS) based in Western Australia and other police tactical groups from around the country, and even the Federal Bureau of Investigation in the United States. In Hollywood films and perhaps even in some real-life military situations, the plan might have been simpler—'just take him out'—but our rules of engagement did not endorse killing except where an offender posed a direct and imminent threat to our own lives, a rule I was certainly glad was firmly in place.

Following the incident in the police station it became an urgent priority to bring the situation to a conclusion as quickly as possible. Packing up our bongos, a colloquial term for getting our gear together, every available operator was sent to the tiny rural town to initiate the arrest phase of an operation which had by now been going for nearly six months. It wouldn't have been hard for the townsfolk to figure out something was about to go down. Although we attempted to remain as covert as possible, the sudden arrival of forty or so fit, serious-looking dudes was no doubt the cause of a new wave of town gossip and rumours, but with little time to spare before the mad scientist returned to town it didn't really matter.

A two-hour tactical briefing was held in the back room of the local bowling club. A briefing is usually limited to the operators involved, but this was like a who's who of upper echelon police. Bosses from every quarter, eager to be involved in an unprecedented Australian operation, were coming out of the woodwork, all keen to have their name associated with something that could, if everything went to plan, be historic in Australian law enforcement. I don't know whether Colin had been watching a few nature documentaries for inspiration, but his plan was to snare the old man as if we were trying to capture a dangerous animal alive. On the crest of a small hill located on the road leading from his property to the town we would set our trap. This allowed us to be a safe distance from him if he decided to go ahead with his intention to detonate the device on seeing the police. His psychological profile and extreme level of paranoia led us to believe he'd have no hesitation, given half the chance.

On the day before he was due to travel to town for his appointment with the station sergeant we were going to place barbed wire across the opposite side of the crest on the road to stop his progress. The sides of the road, hidden in thick bushland, were a perfect place to construct obstacles to block his escape in either direction. These obstacles were set in three stages. The first stage was a 300-metre length of wire placed on either side of the road, which would form a low-lying maze designed to trip and hinder progress. The second stage was an equivalent length of detonation cord, a small-yield explosive that was not designed to maim but merely to be used as a means of distraction if he attempted to go that way. The third stage was a temporary eight-foot fence covered in foliage so it couldn't be seen from the road. All these measures were simply a precaution. We wanted to make sure he couldn't get close to any operators on the flanks of the road when he eventually realised he couldn't go forward. To finalise the entrapment, a camouflaged APC was going to drag another string of barbed wire across the road behind him after he passed, thus completing the makeshift human cage. With everybody out of sight, hidden in the bush behind protective screens or safely dug into makeshift foxholes, a hidden speaker would relay the instructions we wanted him to follow. Brilliant in its simplicity, but complicated in its execution, this plan was the only way we could arrest the old man while keeping him—and everyone else—safe.

During the briefing we were informed by a member of the NSW Police Bomb Squad of the likely result if the device was detonated.

'It will more than likely take his head off at the shoulders with severe damage to the torso. The blast radius will be about eighty metres for a device that size. Anyone not under cover within that range can expect a few holes in them.'

I'd seen the effects of high explosives on a body a few years before when I was stationed on the New South Wales–Victorian border. An employee of the Australian Defence Industries complex at Mulwala, forty kilometres east of where I worked, had a very bad day, mixing the commercial-grade high explosive Pentolite in the wrong proportions and causing a massive explosion that I heard and felt while sitting in my office. Not surprisingly, the explosion caused total devastation of the building and killed the occupant inside. When I arrived at the scene it was purely to assist the forensics team as they picked up and documented as many pieces of the deceased as possible—a difficult task, considering our search and subsequent recovery only yielded 28 kilograms of the deceased's 120-kilogram body, the biggest piece being a seared section of his back that looked more like a large pork roll than part of a human body. Perhaps because the remains didn't really resemble a human being, I felt no remorse or sadness. I just put it down to the bizarre nature of the job—it was one of those things that cops and other emergency personnel see in their work every day. Suffice to say I had a good idea what to expect if that time came.

The day after the briefing was trap construction day. The old man was due for his appointment the following morning. My major task was to dig a foxhole deep enough to conceal myself and another operator, just in front of the stop point, forty metres or so from where we estimated he'd stop. Having never been in the army, this was my first foxhole, but it wasn't exactly rocket science. Dig a hole, put the dirt from the hole in front of it to make a mound and then cover the mound with leaves so that it doesn't look like someone has just dug a hole . . . simple. With all the preparations completed we headed back to town for a well-earned beer in our rooms.

Waking early the next morning to start on the final preparations I could sense a strange assortment of feelings in the air. Some of the more gung-ho members of our group were looking forward to the possibility of getting some target practice on the old man if the opportunity presented itself—some even commenting that it was 'hunting day'—but most, like me, were hoping the matter would be resolved peacefully, and none more so than Colin, who would be coordinating the operation.

Loading into numerous 4WDs we travelled the fifteen or so minutes out of town to the stop point, where I noticed the dirt road had been soaked courtesy of an overnight thunderstorm. *Maybe the gods are trying to tell us something*, I thought as I walked to my foxhole, only to see that the rain had washed a great deal of dirt back into the hole. Luckily, we still had a few hours to go before the old man was due, so I had plenty of time for running repairs. Wearing standard-issue army camouflage clothing, body armour and a Kevlar helmet, I grabbed my M4 after adjusting my foxhole and settled in with Benny, one of the sergeants from our unit.

'Whaddya reckon, Benny?'

'About what, Horse?'

'Is this bloke gonna turn up or what?'

'They reckon he will. Hey, where's the cam paint for your face?'

'I hate that shit, Benny. If I wanted to wear make-up I would have joined the army.'

Benny just laughed. We continued to chat about nothing for the next few hours until my earpiece crackled sharply.

'All teams, this is Charlie. We are standing down. He's not coming today.'

Not bothering to ask why, Benny and I grabbed our equipment from the hole and walked onto the roadway to wait for a ride back into town. I watched as guys in cam gear emerged from their own positions of cover and made their way toward us. Within a few minutes a group of twenty or so operators were milling around waiting to be picked up and ferried back into town. When we got there we had a quick debrief. Colin explained that because it had rained the old man was unable to ride his bike on the slippery dirt roads, and we'd have to do it all again tomorrow.

The routine the next morning was much like the previous day, with the same uncertainty hanging in the air. It had rained again overnight but it wasn't as severe as the previous night's storm, auguring well for us getting the job done safely and going back home. The plan hadn't changed. Our snipers in the OP would give us a heads-up when the old guy was leaving his property, giving us about two minutes to prepare before he got to the top of the crest and saw that the other side was blocked.

Negotiators would speak to him through the hidden speaker, almost as if he were being spoken to by the burning bush, and then we'd give him instructions on what to do next. Once again, Benny and I concealed ourselves in the foxhole, with a similarly placed team on the opposite side of the road. Also concealed in the bush, on the flanks, were several operators at set intervals, ensuring we had the ground covered. In the middle of the road on the outside of the barbed wire was a marked police vehicle, so the old man would be under no illusion as to who surrounded him.

We were expecting him to get to the stop point at around 11 am, as his appointment had been confirmed at the local police station at 11.30 am. The time approached but the air of built-up expectation began to wane as we hadn't heard anything from the OP. Minutes ticked by and another false alarm seemed imminent. Most of the boys began to relax, taking off their helmets and getting comfortable. We were sure we were in for a long afternoon. Knowing I'd have at least two minutes' notice if anything were to happen, I jumped out of my foxhole and walked to the police vehicle about fifteen metres away. I took my body armour and helmet off and hung them on the open door before sitting in the comfort of the passenger seat. I was soon joined by Larry, a mate of mine with whom I always shared a joke.

'Is he gonna turn up, Laz?' I asked him.

'He'd better, Horsey, otherwise they're gonna have to get us some more TA.'

TA, or travelling allowance, is a cash payment given to police when they are on a job away from their normal place of work. It is used to cover accommodation and meal costs and is always the first subject mentioned when there's the possibility of an extended operation.

'They won't do that. We'll have to get it when we get home,' I said.

'Ah, fuck. I hate it when that happens,' Larry replied.

I had to laugh—here we were, lying in wait to arrest a guy with a bomb strapped to his chest and several loaded pistols in his belt, and Larry was worried about the money we were missing out on! I was just hoping we didn't have to kill the old guy. Somehow sensing my thoughts, Larry asked, 'Have you ever shot anyone, Horsey?'

'No, mate.'

'Me neither. Have you ever seen anyone shot dead?'

'Yep.'

'While you worked here?'

'No, when I was in the dog squad in '95.'

'What happened?'

'I went to a violent domestic. I was the only car in the area so I rocked up by myself. I was going to wait for other cars to come but I heard a massive fight going on so I went in. When I got inside a woman yelled at me, "He's upstairs! He's upstairs!" When I got up the stairs and started to open the door to one of the bedrooms, a teenage boy blew his head off with a shotgun. There was shit everywhere. I don't remember anything after that.'

'Fuck me!' Laz exclaimed, not expecting me to come out with a story like that.

We both sat in silence.

I'd never really thought about that incident since it happened but before I could ponder any further, or ask Larry the same question he'd asked me, a nervous voice barked over the radio. 'Urgent! Target is three hundred metres away!'

'Oh, shit!' Larry and I said almost simultaneously as we leapt out of the police vehicle. We only had a matter of seconds before the motorised bicycle would be upon us. I'd learned to put my body armour and accessories on very quickly in the past but never under this much pressure, especially when I could hear the small cylinder engine of the old bloke's bike getting louder by the moment. Putting my gear on in record time, I ran to the foxhole and jumped in, putting on my helmet just as the old man's head appeared over the crest of the road. He slowed as he approached the stop point. A confused expression came across his face as he saw a police car on the road with nobody near it. From my vantage point, about forty-five metres from where he'd stopped, I could see his bewilderment turn to anger as he searched around for something or someone to take his frustrations out on. Then the burning bush began to speak.

'This is the police! You are surrounded and you cannot escape.'

'Where are ya, ya bastards?' the old man said as he turned in circles.

'Put down your weapons and step away from the bike.'

Unable to get a bead on anyone around him, he stood for a few seconds before a look of dejection came over him. He knew that with nothing to shoot at, or even take with him if he detonated the bomb, it was worthless for him to continue. He looked back at his bike and started to pace around like a lion stuck in a rather large cage. I could see he was contemplating his next move. Finally, after several tense minutes, with his head no doubt looming large in the sights of the snipers' rifles, he placed the first of his three loaded pistols carefully on the ground.

'Okay, mate. Now we want you to disarm the pipe bomb and place it on the ground near the pistols and step well away from them. Do you understand?'

'Yeah, I'm not fucking stupid.'

Flicking the switch on the bomb to the 'off' position, he then pulled down the upper half of his overalls and removed the strap holding the device onto his chest. A few seconds later he placed it on the ground, stepping away as instructed.

'Okay, mate, thanks for that. Now we need you to take off your clothes.'

'You fuckin' what?'

I laughed as quietly as I could at his response to what must have seemed an odd request. He stood for a few seconds with a look of total disbelief on his face and proceeded to take off his clothes. Thirty seconds later, the surreal sight of a naked sixty-odd-year-old man standing in the middle of the road was something to behold.

'He's not in bad nick for an old fella, Benny,' I commented.

'Yeah, he looks fitter than me.'

Buck naked, he walked around, looking at the ground, still appearing to think about how he could get out of the situation. The unseen voice spoke again.

'Now walk back down the road toward your place. You will be met there by some police. Do it now.'

'Geez, you're a bunch of bad bastards, aren't ya?' he said as he walked over the small crest and out of sight.

The rest of us relaxed as we waited for the all clear to tell us that he was safely in custody. When it came through we emerged from our concealment until the radio crackled once again.

'Everybody stay where they are. The bomb squad is on its way to check the device.'

Still in our foxhole I turned to Benny.

'What happened to the early call from the OP that he was leaving?'

'I don't know.'

'Fucking snipers!' I said with disbelief.

Although a rumour circulated afterwards that the sniper in the OP had fallen asleep, we never found out what had really happened. Once on the scene, the bomb tech decided that picking up the homemade explosive would not be a wise move, so the experts laid some other explosives around the device and moved everybody back so they could detonate the whole lot. Standing about 400 metres up the road we watched as the pipe bomb and the initiating explosives went up in an immense detonation. The all clear was given and, as we inspected the hole, it soon became apparent the old fella was one hell of a bomb maker!

Back in town, Colin's expression was one of pure relief. The pressure of the past few months, knowing he was responsible for the safety of so many people, including the old man, had weighed heavily on him and it was clear this burden had taken its toll. In the aftermath many people stepped in to try to take some credit for the result but Colin, humble as ever, smiled and took it in his stride. Six months later, one of the sergeants from the unit won an Australian Police scholarship to the United States to address a number of other police agencies, including the FBI, all on the back of a case study conducted on the incident. He hadn't even been involved in the operation.

Like I said, my mate told me I'd be lucky to get through the coppers and not come out a hypocrite.

15

What Am I Doing Here?

By 2003 I'd gained enough experience to begin taking on the role of team leader on high-risk jobs, not so much as a promotion but as a consequence of being the most senior person on a shift. On a particularly busy day in March our team was called to a shopping centre near Bass Hill in Sydney's south-west to assist Crime Squad detectives planning to arrest a gang of guys about to do an armed robbery at a local bank. Unbeknown to the would-be offenders, we knew where and when the stick-up was going to happen, courtesy of some well-placed phone taps, so we took up a covert position in a quiet street about two blocks away from the complex. Although we were in an unmarked vehicle we had nicknamed the DOV (short for Discreet Observation Van), the intelligence gained from the phone taps indicated that the offenders were very wary of any police presence, so I'd decided to allow plenty of distance between us and the target premises, lest we blow the whole operation. We settled in to wait.

By now, most of us were accustomed to lengthy stretches in the DOV, up to twelve hours at a time, only jumping out at the last second to arrest the target(s). Given the stale air inside consisted largely of body odour and farts, long periods of confinement in the DOV made for an uncomfortable stay, especially during protracted stake-outs on cold winter nights when going to the toilet through a custom-made hole in the floor was a challenge, both physically and mentally. Manoeuvring around five or so bulky bodies all in multiple layers of body armour, overalls, jackets and weapons, combined with the inevitable ribbing from the other lads about shrinkage and stage fright, was an exercise worth avoiding.

Such operations made the DOV a second, albeit uncomfortable, home but luckily this particular stay was short. Being team leader it was my job to collate and disseminate any information coming through from the Command Post (CP) so we could move as quickly as possible, always ready to change our plans at a moment's notice. Intelligence gleaned from the phone taps appeared sound. The gang consisted of five or so males (suspects in a string of violent armed robberies over the previous twelve months) who would be driving an old, run-down red Nissan sedan. Such intel was a luxury we didn't always enjoy.

While we were waiting a little voice in my head said: *If I am still jumping out of vans pointing guns at people when*

I am forty, then something has gone seriously wrong. It was a random thought, but it didn't really surprise me. I'd had thoughts like this before, sudden moments of unhappiness or a vague, unfocused resentment, but I chose to ignore them (after all, I was living the macho dream). I forgot all about my brief flicker of discontent as a real voice crackled in my earpiece.

'Charlie, Alpha One.'

Charlie was the call sign we used to designate the tactical commander of the operation. Situated in the CP, he was the overall boss of proceedings. Usually an operator with the rank of inspector or above, he was located a short distance away from the actual scene, coordinating the operation as well as liaising with local police and/or witnesses to give timely, up-to-date information. As the team leader, or Alpha One, my role was to coordinate the troops on the ground and make decisions based on what was in front of me, working closely with the tactical commander to ensure our goal was achieved.

'Alpha One, standing by,' I said.

'The target vehicle with four heads on board is moving through the car park of the shopping centre.'

'Copy that, Charlie. Are they near the bank?'

'Affirmative, Alpha One.'

'Alpha One to all units. Go! Go! Go!'

Of all the adrenaline rushes associated with this type of work this was the most intense, making the long hours of sitting around in the DOV worthwhile for a few seconds of excitement. It was like a drug and I was an addict.

Not wishing to give ourselves away just yet, the driver of the van drove quickly but cautiously so we could close as much distance as possible between us and the bank without alerting the offenders.

'Where are they?' I asked the driver.

'They just pulled up outside the bank.'

'How far away are we?'

'Ten seconds.'

'Get ready, boys, ten seconds,' I told the other operators in the DOV.

As we prepared to jump out and arrest the offenders at gunpoint the driver suddenly accelerated, causing us to fall backwards toward the rear of the van.

'What's going on?' I asked.

'They didn't go in. They're driving off.'

'Chase them! The detectives want them for conspiracy to commit anyway.'

I hit the 'press to talk' on my radio microphone.

'Alpha One. Charlie.'

'Charlie. Alpha One.'

'They're running. We're pursuing the vehicle now.'

'Copy that, Alpha One. Give us a location when you can.'

'Copy that, Charlie.'

For all the DOV's stealth, a race car it was not.

'Lucky it's only a shit box old Nissan,' I said to the driver.

Too busy concentrating on driving as fast as the DOV would take us (with an extra half-tonne of unsecured human ballast in the rear), he didn't reply. We chased

161

the vehicle around a couple of streets near the shopping complex before it stopped in the driveway of a plain, regular-looking three-bedroom brick-veneer house.

'They just ran inside,' the driver said as we pulled up behind the vehicle.

'Can you tell Charlie where we are?' I asked, not expecting a response.

Piling out of the van the team didn't need to be told their next move, automatically spreading out around the house to contain the offenders inside. When the cordon was in place I shouted, 'This is the police! Come out now!'

There was no direct response but I could hear loud shouting coming from the side of the house. It was Scud. One of our most senior operators, his name fit both his appearance and his demeanour perfectly. Short in stature but with a power lifter's physique, he was also as single-minded and destructive as a missile. We could have also nicknamed him the 'hand grenade'. Just pull the pin and throw him in.

'Get out of there you fucking pricks!' he yelled.

My earpiece crackled once again.

'Charlie, Alpha One?'

'Alpha One, Charlie.'

'Yeah, Horse. We've got the negotiators here. Do you want them down there yet?'

Not wanting to get the negotiators involved unless I absolutely had to I replied, 'Just give us a minute, Charlie.'

Then, instead of negotiating, I delivered an ultimatum.

'All right! If you don't come out now we are coming in there to kick the living shit out of you! Understand?'

Within a few seconds the first offender walked out of the house with his hands behind his head. With my M4 pointed directly at him I shouted, 'Get on the ground! Get on the ground!'

Shortly after, another operator secured his hands with plastic zip ties (easily accessible and portable handcuffs) and removed him from the front lawn. Over the next couple of minutes the process was repeated and the remaining offenders were zipped up without incident or excitement. After the house had been cleared we stood down and moved back to our van.

'How come you didn't want the negs, Horsey?' Scud asked.

'You know what they're like, dude. We'd be here until midnight if they got involved.'

'Fucking negotiators,' he said, shaking his head.

'Besides, I think it was your psycho act down the side of the house that did it.'

We both laughed, but despite the euphoria of a successful operation, the feelings of unhappiness and resentment that had surfaced a short while earlier in the DOV would not go away. On the way back to the base I sat quietly in the passenger seat of a 4WD, unable to shake the sensation that my time with the unit had reached its use-by date. As I couldn't see any alternative, I did my best to shut this knowledge away in the deepest recesses of my mind. It was a way of dealing with trouble I'd become very good at.

Three days later I was working a regular dayshift in our office at the Sydney Police Centre (SPC) in Surry Hills. A goliath of a building, apparently built to withstand the possibility of a bomb attack, it housed a large number of peripheral policing services that supported the regular general-duties police in their everyday work. During the day I walked the short distance from the front door of our office to go out through the security turnstiles for a cigarette. Of more than fifty operators I was one of only three who smoked, not including the many closet smokers who would bum a ciggie when we were out having a drink. Still running and exercising regularly, I'd never had any difficulty keeping up with the others which, in such a competitive environment, would often cause frustration on their part. Iliya was a fellow smoker and when we were on shift together, especially if it was a nice day, we'd sit out the front of the SPC and watch the world go by.

Before reaching the turnstiles I stopped to talk to a couple of guys from the weapons training unit who I'd got to know through using the indoor pistol range downstairs. We were chatting, just around the corner from the building's exit, when I heard a shrieking voice. We'd barely whipped our heads around to investigate when we saw a policewoman run around the corner screaming at us, 'Oh, my God! He's been stabbed!'

Not knowing what she was talking about, and not taking the time to ask, I ran around the corner and saw a guy standing on the other side of the turnstiles, near the exit, wielding a huge kitchen knife. Out of the corner of my eye I saw that one of the special constables, a police security guard, was lying on the floor, blood cascading from between his fingers as he pressed his hand to the side of his neck. Without a second thought I ran at the turnstiles, leapfrogged them and confronted the offender, but as soon as I got close he lunged toward me with the knife.

'Back off,' he said in a surprisingly calm manner.

Realising I didn't have any weapons on me and that I was only wearing a pair of dark blue police overalls, I backed off. Still keeping an eye on the guy I ran over to the special constable and checked his belt, grabbing an expandable baton from its sheath. In the moment it took me to grab the baton the guy walked calmly out of the front sliding doors of the building and down the front steps. By the time I got outside he was standing just off the steps, in the forecourt of the SPC, facing me with the knife in his right hand. As soon as I'd got a bead on him I ran like a man possessed down the steps toward him.

'Put the knife down!' I yelled.

Before he had a chance to respond I launched myself from the third or fourth step with all the power I could muster, raising the baton above my head and striking him on the wrist, just above the hand holding the knife. My momentum carried me well past him. Turning around, I half-expected his whole hand to be lying on the ground, I'd hit him that hard. I was wrong. Not only had I apparently inflicted little damage, he was still confidently brandishing the knife. Surprised he was showing no sign of pain, I took a different tack.

'Mate, put the knife down now!' I said, taking up a position about two metres away from him, baton poised above my head to strike again if necessary. 'Put the fucking knife down now!'

Without speaking, he turned and started to walk from the building forecourt across Goulburn Street toward Riley Street. The area where I'd struck his wrist had already become a bulging lump, confirming I had actually caused some damage, albeit not enough to stop him.

How the fuck is this guy still holding this knife? I thought in amazement as I followed him.

Steve, one of the guys I'd been talking to before the stabbing, had joined me in the pursuit and now flanked the guy on one side, aiming his Glock while I walked two metres behind waiting for a chance to tackle him.

'Put the knife down!' Steve repeated a number of times.

Nearing the corner of Albion Street, I knew he only had to turn left and walk a few more metres before he was in the middle of Oxford Street, one of Sydney's busiest pedestrian areas, and then the shit would really hit the fan. When he got to the corner I took my chance. Running the last few metres, I grabbed him from behind in a bear hug, pinning his arms against his side so the knife could not be used to harm anyone. With the adrenaline coursing through my system it was easy to control the slightly built young man and, in a tackle that would have got me suspended for life in any football code, I picked him up like a rag doll and drove him into the pavement with my full weight falling onto him. Within a few seconds Steve and a couple of other cops arrived, helping to handcuff, search and pick up the now profusely bleeding guy to take him back to the SPC. Walking him back down to the scene of the stabbing I was angry. It wasn't just that he'd stabbed a work colleague—I could feel an uncontrollable and inexplicable rage burning within me which had no doubt contributed to the ferocious manner of the arrest. When we got back to the front doors of the SPC we handed him over to some general-duties police who by now had begun to mill around the area, concerned for the welfare of the guard. As I walked back inside I saw Colin crouching over the guard and holding his head.

'How is he, Colin?' I asked.

He just shook his head with an 'I don't think he's gonna make it' expression. The large kitchen knife had gone a long way into the left side of the guard's neck, near his collarbone, resulting in massive blood loss. His grey-looking skin and lifeless posture did not fill me with confidence. Seeing as Colin and a number of other police were working on him I didn't stand around to watch, preferring to wander outside to finish my interrupted cigarette. Standing outside puffing away I realised I'd been on autopilot during the whole incident, not actually stopping to think my actions through before committing to them—a product of many hours spent doing emergency response training. Despite this training, the massive dose of adrenaline that floods the body when rapid action is required had given me a slight case of the shakes as it worked through my system: it was most noticeable as I struggled to light the long-awaited ciggy.

When I did manage to light it I sucked deeply, letting the smoke linger in my lungs before expelling it in an exaggerated sigh. I managed a few more drags before people started coming over and patting me on the back—a nice gesture, I supposed, but not really necessary. Within a few minutes the paramedics arrived and the guard was stabilised and rushed to hospital for emergency surgery. I would later hear on the nightly news that the surgeon who operated on him said the victim was 'the closest person he had seen to death without actually dying'.

Later that afternoon, after we'd answered the obligatory questions from detectives who wanted to know our version of the events, the Police Commissioner, Ken Moroney, came down to see me, Steve and a couple of other police who had helped to arrest the offender. I'd always liked the commissioner and in the few times I'd met him he'd always come across as a sincere person who cared deeply for the men and women under his charge.

'Thank you for what you did today,' he said as he addressed the group. 'I'm going to recommend that you receive bravery awards for this.'

In the thirteen years I'd been in the cops I'd noticed that many of my fellow police had an apparent fascination for collecting awards, some of them even going so far as to recommend themselves for recognition. When the commissioner suggested this possibility, I replied, 'Thanks, boss, but it's really nothing more than what other police do every day.'

It wasn't false modesty. I actually believed the job we did in the Tactical Operations Unit was safer than what many of the general-duties police faced every day in the field. We had the benefit of state-of-the-art equipment, heavy-duty firepower and specialised tactics—none of which the normal police had at their disposal when the shit hit the fan.

A couple of days after the incident I walked into the meal room for the morning briefing, whereupon I was presented with a certificate that one of the boys had made up—a laminated A4 sheet of paper with my photograph and the title *Employee of the Month* on it. It was a much appreciated gesture from a group who didn't give compliments easily and something I valued more than the bravery commendation I'd receive in the coming months.

16

A Fine Line

About a month after the stabbing we were deployed to a residence in Sydney's south-western suburbs as part of a joint taskforce targeting drug offenders. It was a standard-looking premises, another three-bedroom brick-veneer place. I was part of the perimeter team and took up a position behind the back fence. My job, along with another eight guys spread around the sides and front of the house, was to covertly surround the place to prevent any would-be escapees. Once we were in our allocated positions and the perimeter was secure the 'alpha' or entry team entered the house to execute the early-morning search warrant. We heard the familiar shouts of 'with me' and 'clear' coming from inside the house before the six-man entry team eventually walked out the back door to search a garage at the rear.

No sooner had they set foot in the backyard than a pair

of pit bull terriers, who had been quietly hiding behind the garage, lunged at the team, obviously not impressed with the intrusion into their territory. The two dogs threw themselves at the boys time and time again, trying to get under their handheld shields to sink their teeth into some flesh. Even after being covered from head to tail in pepper spray (a deterrent which usually worked a treat on vicious dogs), they continued their assault and eventually repelled the much larger two-legged invaders, who made a hasty retreat back to the relative comfort of the house.

I had spent several years as a police dog handler and, though my understanding of dog psychology was rudimentary at best, I wasn't prepared to let these dogs dictate where we could and could not go.

'We can't let those dogs win,' I said to Dave.

'Don't do it, Horsey, are you fucking nuts?'

'I've never met a dog yet I can't dominate!' I chirped confidently as I started to climb the flimsy, six-foot-tall Colorbond fence, not considering the effect my fully laden weight of 130 kilograms might have on it. Looking over the top I saw the two dogs near the back door of the house. They had been barking at the alpha team but had obviously heard the noise I made as I climbed the fence and now, quietly, with a new focus, they eagerly eyed me off.

I imagined what the two of them would say if they could talk:

''Ere, what's this bloke up to then?' the first dog would mutter in a broad Cockney accent, amazed that someone would be crazy enough to have another go.

'Don't know, Gov, but he looks tasty, innit,' his mate would reply.

'Right then, geezer, I reckon we let on that we're scared of this git. Make him come in the yard, know what I mean?' the first dog would add with a hefty laugh.

'Surely he ain't that stupid,' the second dog would say as it shook its head.

He was.

I was.

I screamed like a banshee at the top of my voice.

'Heeeeyyaaaarrrrr!'

Seeing the dogs flinch slightly at the sight of a crazy madman coming into their territory I thought: *got 'em.* I really did believe that by being crazier and more aggressive than they were, I'd show them that I was top dog, and they would submit. I'd used the same tactic only about a month before, when two Rottweilers bailed up some operators in the backyard of another house at a similar job. It had worked perfectly then, and it worked perfectly this time as well—until I was in a precariously balanced position on top of the fence. I was swinging my legs over, ready to jump into the yard, when both dogs launched themselves at me, embedding their teeth into the fleshy parts of my lower right leg.

'Ah, fuck!' I yelled as their canines sank further and further in.

In a scene reminiscent of the *Keystone Cops* I was balancing unsteadily on my arse atop the fence with both feet inside the yard, two dogs biting into my right leg while Dave was hanging onto my belt from behind to stop me falling in and getting completely mauled. I threw my M4 back over the fence and grabbed an expandable baton from my over-vest. I saw another operator, Steve, aiming his M4 in the direction of my leg.

'Don't shoot! Don't shoot!' I yelled at him.

Despite the fact I had two huge pit bulls hanging off my leg and regardless of how much pain I was in, I didn't want to see these dogs killed when they were, in actuality, just doing their job—plus I wasn't sure how good Steve's aim was!

Thirty seconds seemed like a lifetime but I eventually smacked one of the dogs in the middle of the forehead, causing him, and his mate, to let go, allowing me to scramble unceremoniously back to the safe side of the fence.

Back on safe ground I looked at the ragged bottom of my overalls. Lifting the tattered strips of material revealed that the dogs' teeth had left several deep puncture wounds in my right calf and I was bleeding profusely. The reward for my morning's work was an orchestra of laughter from the boys. Amazed I'd avoided a complete mauling I turned to Dave with a nervous smile.

'There's a fine line between tough and dumb and I think I just stepped over it!' I said.

'Mate, you didn't step over it, you jumped,' Dave replied. 'We'd better get the ambulance.'

'No, it'll be fine, Dave,' I said, with false bravado. My leg really hurt like hell but I couldn't show it, not with all the boys watching on. Knowing the request for an ambulance would be met with questions about why it was required, I was reluctant to make a fuss, but Dave was insistent, unable to contain his joy at making this embarrassing situation known to everyone else. Laughing as he spoke, he contacted the command post via the radio.

'Bravo 2, Charlie.'

'Go ahead, Bravo 2.'

'Could we get an ambulance to the rear of the target house? We have a dog bite that needs attention.'

'Copy that, Bravo 2. We heard a ruckus around the back there. Is everybody okay?'

'Yes, Charlie. Horse just had a run in with some dogs.'

'Copy that.'

An ambulance always accompanied our operations—albeit normally for more serious reasons—and as it pulled into a side street near the back of the house, I limped over to get some treatment. My overalls were hanging by a thread, my boots were ripped and I had a puncture in my leg the size of a twenty cent piece. I reckon I must have looked like Principal Ed Rooney in the final scene of *Ferris Bueller's Day Off*.

Despite the pain it was a little hard to take myself seriously. Even the ambulance officer had a smirk on his face as he treated the wound. Knowing the story had filtered through to the other emergency services made an even great dent in my ego.

It wasn't long before my ego bounced back, though. Along with eight other instructors I was chosen to oversee the selection of a new intake of tactical operator applicants. In a perverse kind of way it was payback time. I still had very distinct memories of my selection courses and here I was about to be on the other side of the proverbial fence. Now you would think, considering my experiences, that I would go easy on the candidates and not inflict the same torture as had been inflicted on me, but in the macho, testosterone-fuelled world of the TOU that wasn't how it worked. If anything, I was going to be worse. Remember those teachers at school who loved to inflict punishment on the kids? You just know they were bullied when they were at school and they see their position of authority as the perfect chance for revenge.

At the beginning of the course the senior instructor approached me.

'Horsey, we'd like you to be a real prick during this course. Really put the pressure on them to see how they react.'

'No sweat. Do I have to subscribe to actor's equity?' I asked jokingly.

'You're kidding, aren't you? You'll get off on it.'

I knew he was right. Although I'd be performing—pretending to be something I didn't really believe I was—there was a strange kind of thrill that came from the power associated with the role, and I was primed to really get stuck into the new candidates.

I was to become the new Figjam!

When the course began with a day of physical tests at various venues around Sydney Harbour, so did the taunts and intimidation. I effectively became that which I had railed so heavily against only a few years before. One particular candidate, a shy, timid-looking guy, seemed out of place in the group from the moment he arrived and I singled him out for some special attention because I thought he was an easy target.

'What are you doing here?' I asked him early in the day.

'I want to help the people of New South Wales.'

I almost fell over laughing, not remembering I had searched for a similar answer years earlier.

'I don't know how much help you'll be to the people of New South Wales—you'll be lucky to see the end of today, sunshine,' I said sarcastically.

At the end of the first day the exhausted candidates were put on a bus and driven to a venue in Goulburn that would become their home for the next seven days. On the bus they were given puzzles and complicated quizzes to complete before they reached their destination, all while listening to eardrum-bursting levels of heavy metal music. Loud, continuous, fast-paced music accelerates the effects of sleep deprivation, as it gives the mind no time for respite. It's a popular method of torture—most famously used in interrogations conducted by US Military Psy Ops (Psychological Operations) in Iraq and Guantanamo Bay as a way of breaking down an individual's resistance. We used it merely to disrupt the candidates' concentration and increase the pressure they felt.

Apart from a few minor differences, the candidates were subjected to the same stock-standard endless series of push-ups, sit-ups and running drills I had experienced just a few years ago, only this time I was handing out the punishment. I knew I was only playing a role, but I still felt a bizarre pleasure in ranting at the candidates, like

I was releasing pent-up energy. Every time I shouted at them I actually felt good for a short while afterwards.

In the middle of the second day the candidate I'd singled out for attention a day earlier came up to me.

'Excuse me, staff. I'd like to quit.'

'Why is that?' I said to him in a very stern manner.

'It's not for me.'

I couldn't help but feel respect for the guy—he had the guts to be honest. I'd watched him going through the physical torture, noting that he seemed fit enough, and I suspected that he had the tenacity to get through the biggest shock to his system that he'd probably experience in his life. Softening in my demeanour, I began speaking to him like a normal person again.

'That's a shame, mate. Do you have any injuries that we can get the paramedic to have a look at?'

'No. I just want to go home.'

'Fair enough. Best of luck in whatever path you choose.'

'Thank you, staff.'

'You can call me Horse now. Cheers.'

After he left the compound the facade went straight back up, and my tough-guy act actually intensified over the next few days. Truth be told, I was probably worse than Figjam! By the end of the week, having got so much enjoyment out of playing this role, I began to wonder whether I had really been acting or if it was just a convenient excuse to vent my anger at the unsuspecting blokes who had signed up.

A part of me seemed to crave authority, wanting to feel important—and being a police officer didn't seem to have satisfied that craving. I'd spent so many years perfecting my macho facade that I hadn't developed the skills I needed to deal with my emotional problems. Instead I just suppressed them, stuffing my feelings of pain, sadness, discontent or anger deep down inside. Here it was coming out but not in a healthy way; I wasn't actually dealing with my problems I was simply transferring them onto these new candidates.

17

Wild West

The game of domination wasn't limited to the workplace—
it went on out of hours too. I rated myself pretty highly,
and no longer needed to wear tactical equipment to feel
bulletproof, especially when in the company of other guys
from the unit. Together we were much like a gang that
has developed its own culture and pecking order, and
we often went out drinking and socialising together. The
combination of bravado and alcohol was a sure-fire recipe
for conflict.

On one such occasion about twenty of us went to the
Hunter Valley for a buck's weekend of drinking, male
bonding and a bit of mischief, and on the Saturday night
we decided to go to an Irish bar in the main street of
Cessnock. As we entered the bar it was obvious we stood
out like the proverbial dog's balls. The bar was patronised
by a large contingent of miners from a nearby colliery

who had the tough, no-nonsense look of the typical blue-collar worker. I don't know if they knew we were cops but a large group of fit-looking blokes, dressed in clothes more in sync with city nightlife, entering *their* bar seemed enough to warrant their attention.

In the early part of the night we kept our distance, watched from afar by the other patrons. Without too much alcohol in us we managed to keep to ourselves, but we became louder and louder and more animated as our intoxication increased. Around 10 pm a heavy metal band began to play in the main bar. There were a few hundred people in the bar by then, and most were already intoxicated. Watching from the side of the deserted dance floor I could see our presence was attracting the attention of one particular group who were sitting near the front door, diagonally opposite where we were standing. When the band kicked into full gear, belting out a fantastic version of Alien Ant Farm's 'Smooth Criminal', a few of us hit the dance floor to create our own mosh pit. We were jumping around like madmen near the front of the band when a guy who I hadn't seen came onto the dance floor. He was solidly built but much shorter than me and my immediate thought was simply that he was coming to join in the fun, but then I saw that he was carrying a beer. Having worked as a bouncer at busy hotels in the early nineties, I realised from his body language that enjoying the music on the dance floor was the last thing on his mind. Nostrils flared, he puffed out his chest, like a bull squaring off against a matador, and I waited for his warring words.

'You guys think you're special, don't ya?'

'What?' I asked with my hand cupped around my ear, unable to hear him over the loud music.

'You blokes think you're special!' he yelled as loudly as he could.

Why does everybody ask me that? I thought.

Deep down, I knew.

As members of the TOU, we were at the top of the food chain, at least in police circles. We thought we were shit hot, and it was obvious. Our modus operandi was one of intimidation. We'd overwhelm our foe with superior numbers and firepower. This sense of collective superiority was deeply entrenched.

Group elitism was something I'd experienced on many occasions, especially when we were doing training exercises at the Police Academy in Goulburn. On one occasion I remember we were fast-roping from a helicopter into a purpose-built village during a mock counterterrorist exercise. Fast-roping was a quick way to get operators onto the ground in an emergency, sliding down a thick rope suspended from a hovering helicopter, as if it were a fireman's pole. Doing this in front of awestruck police cadets gave us a huge buzz. Seeing ourselves through their eyes, we thought we were pretty special.

But I knew better.

For some years myself and a few other guys who liked to take the piss had talked about getting a recording of the *Benny Hill* theme to play over the loudspeaker of the ERV when we showed up at jobs—after all, we'd seen the so-called elite make all-too-human mistakes on occasions too numerous to count. And whether it was accidentally recreating an episode of *Benny Hill* or the *Keystone Cops* the result was the same: hilarity.

Back in the bar I sternly replied to the guy's loaded question.

'Go away, dickhead.'

My mate Batman slapped the guy's hand away, smashing his glass of beer to the floor. 'Fuck off, mate!' Batty said. As the guy turned and walked back to his own group on the other side of the dance floor, Batty explained himself. 'He was about to hit you with that glass, brother.'

I'd been unable to see the guy's hands because I was standing so close to him, but Batty had seen him getting ready to swing the half-empty glass at my face. In the four years I worked on the door of the Woolloomooloo Hotel near Sydney Harbour I'd seen the result of a broken schooner glass connecting with someone's face many times. It was never a pretty sight.

'Thanks, brother.'

Common sense would have dictated it was time for us to patronise a different hotel, but after several glasses of false courage, we weren't running away. For the next hour or so we continued to drink, keeping a watchful eye on our new adversaries, but as the beat of the music reached moshing levels again we headed once more to the dance floor. Within minutes, a couple of locals joined us and began crashing into us as we bounced. Jumping to the rhythm of Rage Against the Machine's 'Killing in the Name', I was suspended in midair when one of the locals hit me with a shoulder charge that completely knocked me off balance and it was on for young and old.

Within thirty seconds the dance floor was awash with human bodies shoving and pushing. I squared off with the guy who shoulder charged me and, holding on to each other's shirts, we traded punches like a pair of ice hockey players. As we fought I could feel blows raining down on the back of my head. Taking a quick look around, I saw each bloke from our group involved in the melee, every one of them with two or three locals on him, which explained why I was getting hit from every direction. In a throwback to the days of the Wild West, the crowd surged toward the front of the hotel, bursting out through the entrance like they were crashing through a pair of saloon doors.

Out on the street and in the confusion I separated myself from my fellow combatant and looked around for the other guys, trying to avoid further punches or even a glass to the back of my head. I'd seen many large brawls in my police career but this was the first where I wasn't wearing a uniform, giving a whole new perspective to the occasion. As the carnage intensified I heard the familiar wail of approaching police sirens.

'Cops!' Batty yelled.

'Let's get out of here!' I heard another bloke call out.

There was an unwritten rule: if you were ever involved in something while out drinking it was best to avoid being questioned by our own. The police hierarchy were said to take a dim view of off-duty police behaving badly while intoxicated. We weren't going to hang around and find out if this was true. Running up the street, helped along by the taunts of the crowd, we stopped a few blocks away to catch our breath.

'Is everybody here?' I asked, looking around and counting heads to make sure we hadn't left anyone behind.

'That was fucking nuts!' Batty said laughing.

'I reckon!' I said. I laughed too, but I could still feel the adrenaline pulsing through my body—and the nervous energy it brought with it. There was a smear of blood on my shirt, courtesy of a tiny cut to my forehead but, considering what just happened, it was a small price to pay. I looked at Paul, a broad-shouldered bloke with the build of a front row forward, and saw his nose had been badly broken. It was now repositioned at a forty-five-degree angle across his face.

'You all right?' I asked.

'Fuck off,' he responded curtly.

'C'mon, mate, we're on the same side,' I said.

'I'll fight you too, Horsburgh!'

Obviously embarrassed he'd come out of the fracas the worse for wear, Paul was responding with aggression, seeking to reassert dominance, just as I might have if the tables were turned.

'Leave me alone. I gotta straighten this nose,' he added, after several more inquiries as to his wellbeing.

We watched as Paul walked towards the nearest building, put the side of his nose against the corner of a wall and pushed his head against it. After watching his cringe-worthy but unsuccessful efforts to restore his good looks, I decided I'd had enough excitement for the night and started walking back to our hotel, not more than a few blocks away.

Waking up the next morning with a slight headache, I felt the back of my head. There were lumps all over it. 'I suppose that's what happens when you pick fights with miners,' I mumbled to myself.

As the months dragged on, my frustration and apathy at work built, to the point where my utter lack of respect attracted comment. Since coming to the unit I had slowly developed a reputation for not giving a shit about anything, often sneaking off for a sleep on dayshift and, on one occasion, lighting up a cigarette while sitting with my feet on the desk in the main office area, causing the shift supervisor to shoot me a look of disgust and walk out of the room without saying anything. My naps became a source of considerable amusement among some of the boys, who were amazed at my arrogance. Just down the hallway from our office there was a night-shift standdown room and blokes would normally go there for a nap, but I gradually became more and more ambitious, eventually finding a convenient spot under a row of desks in the corner of the office, a bit like George Costanza on *Seinfeld* when he created a personal retreat under his desk while working for the New York Yankees. Although small, it was a comfortable spot, allowing me a few minutes of rest right under the noses of the surrounding hierarchy.

Lying in this place of solitude one day, I heard the unmistakeable voice of our Chief Inspector on the other side of the desk. He was a large, humourless man with whom I'd never gotten on. He had a violent temper, and when provoked his face flushed a fiery red, as if he were a character in a cartoon, earning him his nickname: Tomato Head. I knew I pushed his buttons, having heard through the grapevine that he saw both Iliya and me as troublemakers. I stood up from behind the desk, standing face to face with him—he couldn't have been more than two metres away. Looking him squarely in the eye, I waited for his reaction. The one I got was certainly not the one I expected. Instead of quizzing me about what I was doing, he simply turned, walked back to his office and slammed the door. Bemused by his response I walked into the nearby meal room and started making myself a coffee.

'Benny!' I heard Tomato Head shout to one of the sergeants.

A couple of minutes later Benny, the bloke I'd been in the foxhole with a few years earlier, walked into the meal room.

'He's not happy, Horse.'

'Well why didn't he say something?'

'You know what he's like.'

'I don't really care, Benny. If he wants respect then he can grow some balls and speak to me himself.'

'Mate, I was told to come in here and speak to you.'

'Sorry, mate. I didn't mean to bring you into this.'

'No sweat, just don't do it again when he's around.'

'All right, cheers.'

With work relationships reaching an all-time low, my personal life was also on the way down. My first real relationship since my marriage breakdown was with Sasha, a pretty brunette who seemed to fit the image I'd created for myself over the past few years. She was a fantastic-looking accessory, but deep down I was intimidated by her good looks and couldn't help feeling I was punching above my weight. I wasn't the only one who thought so. When we went out I was often told by all and sundry, 'Man, she's out of your league!'

Being told this only added to an already growing list of insecurities, contributing to my overall dissatisfaction with my life. We were together for about eighteen months, and I hung on tightly, not wishing to be rejected again, but from the very beginning I knew the relationship wasn't going anywhere.

So many blokes I knew went out with girls just because they made good arm candy, without any thought to the more profound aspects of a relationship.

Like joining the cops, I thought going out with a beautiful woman would make me feel powerful and worthy. Unfortunately, it had the opposite effect, and I was stuck running on a treadmill that kept getting faster and faster. Driven by my insecurities I became jealous and possessive—which made Sasha more cautious and secretive, which made me even more jealous and possessive, which made Sasha . . . you get the point.

Feeling vulnerable, but not able to admit it, I sought attention from other girls so that I would have something to hide from Sasha, restoring the balance of power in our relationship, but it didn't work. I was just hurting others as I tried to mask my own hurt and confusion. In the end, my mental pain outweighed the pleasure I got from my relationship with Sasha and I made the choice to break up with her.

Not long after we parted ways I decided to disconnect myself from the ill feeling at work as well, putting in my resignation and heading off, hoping for greener pastures. Although I'd been a police officer almost my entire adult life, and my career was such a huge part of my identity, I convinced myself that it wasn't important. After all, my job had contributed to the breakdown of my marriage (and just about every other relationship I had ever been in) and left me with serious scars—physical and emotional. The decision was an easy one, made even easier because I chose to move to another law enforcement agency. I wouldn't be a cop anymore but I could live with that if I had a more satisfying job and leadership I could respect.

18

Jumping through Hoops

Almost as soon as I walked into the office of a covert venue in Canberra to begin training as an Air Security Officer (ASO), I knew I really hadn't made any significant changes to my career. I'd merely shuffled the deckchairs on a sinking ship.

Filled with several other disgruntled tactical operators from various police agencies around Australia, including seven others from my previous workplace, the room looked and sounded very familiar, with the same sorts of guys I had worked with in Sydney having the same conversations about jobs they had been on or just taking the piss out of each other. It also had the same air of intimidation I had experienced during the SWAT course before the Olympics, mainly because the instructors had been coaxed across to the ASO program from tactical police arenas. Set up to combat the perceived threat of hijacking following the events of 9/11, the ASO program was a specialised branch of the Australian Protective Service (APS), a subsidiary body of the Australian Federal Police (AFP). From the outset it was obvious any experience gained through state police agencies was null and void as the AFP sought to exert its dominance over its new recruits. Before being accepted into the program, many of us from the Tactical Operations Unit had applied for recognition of prior learning, so we wouldn't be required to do the early parts of the course. In any registered training organisation, this is a standard procedure; acknowledging an applicant's skills and previous education benefits both parties. I scrounged around for two weeks to get a mountain of information together—certificates, papers, proofs, et cetera—and so did the other seven guys from the TOU. After collating it all and sending it through for approval, we were informed that our prior learning wouldn't be recognised.

Well why the fuck did they ask? I thought, knowing from experience that when the left hand doesn't know what the right hand is doing there are going to be dramas.

We were required to sit through the APS section of the program for the first eight weeks, learning how to be a police officer all over again. As the ASO component of the program wouldn't even start until we had qualified as APS security officers, it was a monotonous waste of time that dragged on forever. Larry, my mate from Tac Ops, had joined the ASO program twelve months before and was now an instructor.

'Just jump through the hoops, Horsey,' he told me one day.

'I know, brother.'

When the ASO component of the program finally came around it was a welcome relief, as many of us were now able to start training for the reason we'd come here: to become specialist anti-hijacking operators.

Right from the start it was clear that mastering this new discipline wouldn't be too much of a challenge. The methodology and skills were very similar to those we'd learned while undergoing the Air Ops component of the SWAT course. It soon became obvious, too, that many of the instructional staff were a little intimidated by their students. The instructors were mostly regular army or general police, without any sort of tactical background, and they were dealing with a large group of blokes who did have that experience. Apart from the guys from the TOU, there were also a number of ex-SAS operators among the students. It made for a weird dynamic. The instructors appeared to be a little unsure how to handle the situation, and that was confirmed when I overheard one of them ask another instructor, 'How the hell are we gonna teach these guys anything?'

Despite all this, the course flowed on. I was building on old skills as well as learning some new ones, such as the art of Brazilian jiujitsu, but the all-too-familiar *what am I doing here?* questions began to raise their ugly heads again.

'This is the last course I'm ever doing!' I said to Iliya, who had also come across to the program.

'Why's that, Horsey?'

'This joint is no different to where we just left.'

'I know, but just think how cruisy it will be when we finish.'

'That's the scary part. This joint couldn't organise a root in a brothel.'

When the course finished and we were deployed to a covert office near Sydney Airport the true nature of the role was revealed. In the first few months as an operational air marshal I enjoyed sitting in business class, eating business-class food and watching movies on demand, all while travelling to some exotic, and some not so exotic, interstate and overseas locations.

It was easy, almost like semi-retirement with the benefits of travel and a fat pay cheque to boot, but that voice of discontent would not abate. The operators were always playing games, vying for dominance. It was a lot like life at the TOU, but probably even worse, as we spent so much time sitting around doing nothing. The constant bickering and one-upmanship reached levels that were hard to fathom, with grown men running to the AFP's division of Internal Affairs every time they had a grievance, much like a child would run to the teacher if somebody called them a name. Watching the shenanigans from the outside, I refused to get involved. The guys who had previously been tactical operators liked to think they were superior to other members of the team, and this was the cause of many disputes. I tried not to take sides, but when I saw one of my former workmates from the TOU, now a deputy team leader, berate a colleague for wearing denim jeans on a flight, I couldn't remain on the sidelines anymore. When he walked back into his office away from the others I challenged him.

'What the fuck was that all about?'

'He was wearing jeans on a flight yesterday, Horsey. You know that's against regulations.'

'Dude, you know as well as I do it's a stupid rule. What's the big deal?'

'These blokes have no idea. They shouldn't be here.'

'Mate, you have a short memory. I worked with you last week and you wore jeans.'

'That's different.'

'You're kidding me, aren't you? You blokes are acting like bullies in a schoolyard.'

'Fuck off, Horse. These blokes are fucking hopeless.'

'Mate, they passed the same course you did. Does that make you better?'

'I don't rate them.'

'It doesn't matter if you don't rate them, dude. They're our workmates.'

As I watched him storm off with the strops, I knew things would be different at work from now on. I had been that bully on the other side of the fence, but now I found myself defending the guys who simply wanted to do their jobs and go home. They didn't live the life of a tactical guru. They didn't need to because it wasn't required. Word spread through the organisation like wildfire and I was branded a 'traitor' to my past vocation, along with a few others from my old workplace. Not that I really cared.

In an attempt to alleviate some of the problems I applied to become a senior air security officer (SASO) within the organisation, and was accepted. The role of the SASO was to lead a team of ASOs when we were deployed on overseas operations; as team leader, I thought that I would at least be able to try to provide a working environment conducive to employee happiness, even if it was only for the few days of the operation. Despite this elevation in status I continued to watch the games from both within our office and from the ASO coordination team in Canberra, knowing it was only a matter of time before I pulled the pin and left of my own accord. I'd had enough—and then an incident during a training day all but sealed my fate.

With a few flights here and there and very little else to do, training became a monotonous break from the well . . . monotony. The ASO program had been established in response to the events of 9/11, but five years had passed and nothing had happened. While I sat on my many flights around the place I often wondered why we even existed. Sure, Bin Laden had apparently orchestrated the attack using aeroplanes and it had been successful, but the likelihood of him, or anyone else, trying it again was minimal. Even the dumbest terrorist would know that the chance of the same thing succeeding twice was very thin and, pardon the pun, the horse had already bolted. We were working for a tax-sucking leviathan, and the money spent on our salaries needed justification, so with the absence of any real-time operational jobs to perform the organisation resorted to training.

Weekly training was repetitive and counterproductive, with many of the operators often going off sick when they knew a training day was coming up. Every now and then the national training manager would grace us with his presence, flying in under the pretext of imparting his expertise, along with ASOs from around the country. During one of these national training days we were at a pistol range in the city's eastern suburbs, part of the massive Malabar range complex. About forty or so ASOs from around Australia had gathered for a qualification shoot—an exercise designed to ensure we were competent in the use of our Glock pistols. We were always serious when we were on the firing line, but waiting at the back of the range in between shooting sequences always led to a few high jinks, especially when we were joined by some of the other guys from around Australia, many of whom had gone through the same ASO course. Our illustrious national training manager was a strange cookie. A stern man, totally devoid of any sense of humour, he was a typical example of someone who takes themselves way too seriously. During the range practice he would look around disapprovingly if he detected any laughter or noise coming from a seated area some fifty metres away from where he was conducting the range. After everybody rotated through the line to qualify we gathered under the shade to listen to his training debrief.

'Okay. I am going to give this debrief in what I call a shit sandwich,' he began. 'Some good points at the start, some criticisms in the middle and I'll finish on a good note.'

Pretty sound idea, I thought, until he began to tear strips off us. From the get-go he criticised everything: the shooting standard, the attitude, even commenting on some of the guys' clothing. His tirade lasted for a full ten minutes, dotted with 'fuck this' and 'fuck that'. He completely lost it—I don't recall ever seeing such a display. I'd been an instructor for many years and I found the process of teaching others is not one improved through abuse or intimidation. It ticks all the wrong boxes and this guy had a full sheet. At the end of his rant, breathless and red in the face, he did the one thing good instructors always do: asked for feedback. I couldn't resist.

'Where's the good in that?' I asked rather matter-of-factly. He'd promised to start and end with the good points, but all I'd heard was criticism. It wasn't a shit sandwich; it was just shit.

'That's what I'm fucking talking about!' he screamed, presumably referring to my attitude. 'Let's go,' he added, motioning like a pop diva for his small entourage to follow.

He turned around, walked back to his car in a huff and sat inside while we all looked around dumbfounded. Here was a senior member of an organisation that allegedly taught counterterrorism tactics, acting like somebody had just stolen his lollipop, but it did get me thinking: *people storming away from me is becoming a pattern.*

In the months following my run-in with the national training manager, the words 'where's the good in that?' became something of a slogan in the office, with many of the guys who had been treated harshly by the establishment latching onto the rebellious sentiment it expressed. Any notoriety I had gained was short-lived, though. I pulled up stumps once again and decided to head to Iraq at the urging of my mate Batman.

Carol, the administration assistant attached to our office, was the real brains behind the operation. Nothing happened without Carol's knowledge and if any problems needed solving she was the go-to person. Funny isn't it; dozens of macho guys trying to prove how good they are but one woman runs the whole show and, without her, the whole castle would crumble. I liked Carol, she was honest and knowledgeable. We'd always have a good chat while having a cigarette outside. Walking into her office one Friday I said, 'I'm leaving, Carol. What do I need to fill out so I can quit?'

'You're what?' she said, exasperated.

'I've had enough. I've been offered a contractor's job in Iraq.'

'Oh, Horsey, no.'

'Sorry, Carol. You know I'm not happy here.'

The tone of my voice told her that I'd made my mind up and Carol knew me well enough not to push the point.

'All right,' she said reluctantly. 'When are you going?'

'Tuesday.'

'Oh, shit! They're going to have kittens in Canberra! You're supposed to give two weeks' notice.'

'Too bad. I'm leaving on a plane on Tuesday.'

'Okay,' she said with a chuckle. 'I'll organise it.'

'Thanks, Carol. You're the best.'

Within an hour Carol had cut through all the red tape and my resignation was rushed through. A few days later I boarded an Emirates flight to Dubai to pick up a transferring flight into Baghdad.

19

The Professor

'You're either guided by your soul or driven by your ego!' the Professor said matter-of-factly.

'What was that?' I said, my mind a thousand miles away.

'You're either guided by your soul or driven by your ego!' he repeated.

I looked at this elderly man and knew I had just heard a profound truth.

Despite the oppressive heat and choking dust of a Middle Eastern midsummer's day, and still feeling a little shaken in the aftermath of the previous night's mortar attack, I knew I'd just heard something meaningful. Sitting just outside the relative comfort of our air-conditioned admin building, sharing the pleasure of a coffee and a few cigarettes after a long day's training in the heat, we looked out over the expanse of desert. The Professor, as he'd affectionately become known within our group, spoke in a calm, peaceful manner that was a complete contrast to the chaos and confusion surrounding us.

He was an enigma. A quietly spoken man of about sixty years, short in stature with a bald head and a pot belly, he had taught English at the University of Baghdad for thirty or so years prior to the arrival of the coalition. During my time at An-Numinayah I'd only spoken briefly to him, mainly in his capacity as one of our interpreters, but I'd noticed he always moved quietly and gracefully among us while he did his job. There was something indescribable about him. A confidence or an unhurried manner that made it seem like everything happening around him was only a temporary arrangement.

Even the weather didn't faze him. It was approaching midday. The mercury was already nigh on fifty degrees and, despite the low humidity, the heat was stifling. It took my breath away, but not the Professor's. He appeared to be in his element, not even cracking a sweat, a slight smile on his face even indicating that he was enjoying the high temperature. Our view across the sun-baked asphalt shimmering in the midday sun and windswept flatlands that kicked up a never-ending supply of dust was broken only by a number of poorly designed and constructed buildings.

'You're either guided by your soul or driven by your ego.'

I let his words sink in, trying to comprehend what he was saying. I sipped on my coffee and dragged back on yet another Gauloises. He spoke again.

'Do you know these words about the soul and the ego?'

'No.'

'They are from the Qu'ran.'

'I didn't know that.'

'Like the Bible, it is a book of peace.'

'I haven't read either of them.'

'Both of these books have been distorted over time. Just like the legend of the hanging gardens of Babylon. Do you know this?'

'I have heard of them, yes.'

'Despite what many people think, it was only a few pots hanging around a garden.'

I laughed at his interpretation of history. Not because I thought he was wrong but because he had so casually dismissed what was widely regarded as an ancient wonder of the world. With just a few words, he had rejected conventional wisdom that had been passed down over thousands of years.

'Do you enjoy doing this?' he now asked.

'Enjoy what?' I replied with a degree of naivety.

'Being here?'

'Of course.'

'Is that the truth?'

I don't know whether he picked up signals from my body language or if I gave him clues in my manner of speech but his question triggered something that rattled my mind like a pinball machine on tilt. In that moment I became painfully aware that what I thought was true and the way I had been acting were polar opposites. I could finally hear the little voices of concern that had been crying for so many years with absolute clarity.

'No. Not really,' I said.

'Then what are you doing here?'

'I came here to help rebuild your country.'

'Bullshit . . . you came here for the money!'

I looked at him with surprise, partly because of his use of English slang, but more so because he recognised that my defiant reply was merely an attempt to shield myself and defend my actions: 'Don't question me, I'm here to help!' Yes, I'd accepted a contract to deliver training to the newly formed Iraqi Police, but I *was* really only there for the money; bombs and bullets for the princely sum of US$550 a day.

'Fuck, you don't miss a trick do you?' I said.

'You are only tricking yourself but at least you have the balls to admit it.'

'What do you mean?' I asked, surprised again by his use of Aussie lingo.

'I've had the chance to speak with many of the contractors who come through here and you are the first one to give me what I consider to be an honest answer. All we have is our integrity, so what you do with it now is up to you.'

I was taken aback by his words, and even more by his timing. It was only the night before, in the moments before the second mortar explosion, that I had started thinking about these sorts of questions for myself, and I'd been preoccupied by them all day.

'What do you mean by integrity?' I asked.

'Well, if you are not happy here, then you are out of your integrity.'

'I don't understand.'

'If we are living with integrity we are whole. If we are not whole we cannot be happy.'

'What do you mean by "whole"?'

'If you are doing something that does not agree with your personal morals or values, then you are not being true to yourself, therefore you cannot be whole.'

I finally got what the Professor was talking about. He'd done something for me that I'd needed someone to do for so long: he had laid things down in simple form; no fuss, no bullshit. For as long as I could remember I'd been questioning myself, constantly querying whether I was making the right decisions, doing the right thing, living the right life, but I had continually suppressed these thoughts because I was caught up in an ego-obsessed masquerade. I was addicted to adrenaline in the same way that other people are dependent on drugs or alcohol, and the addiction was just as powerful. Without fully understanding how or why, I'd been experiencing a form of discord; what I was doing and how I was acting were in complete conflict with my inner thoughts and values. I craved peace yet here I was in a war zone. I had seen the Iraqi people struggling to live day to day, hoping they would one day find their own peace, and yet as a part of the coalition I was contributing to the problem.

'I take it that if we are not living within our integrity then it creates conflict?' I asked.

'Yes. Acting within our integrity is a form of soul guidance that allows us to accept what happens without pushing against it. Conflict on the other hand is an ego-driven response which fuels the need to prove you are right.'

'So does that have to do with our belief systems?'

'Yes it does—you are learning quickly! If we have a belief system which says that our way is right, then we will fight very hard to prove it. Do you understand?'

'Yes.'

It was all falling into place.

I realised I was totally unhappy with where I was and what I was doing, and squashing these thoughts and feelings down had only caused me increasing frustration. This dissatisfaction contributed to behaviour which, even in a high-risk work environment, was considered to be unusually dangerous. In the previous ten years I'd built a reputation as an extreme risk-taker (as many scars will attest), as well as being highly confrontational with people in positions of authority. In all fairness, this notoriety was well founded.

'You only need to look at what is happening around us to see that,' the Professor added.

'So you think that individual integrity has got something to do with the war?' I queried.

'Think about it. One group of people believe they have the answers to everybody's problems while another is resisting because they have the opposite view. It is as simple as that.'

'I see what you mean—it feels a lot like a battle between Christians and Muslims, doesn't it?'

'It does and it has been going on for a long time. The Americans think their way of democracy is what we need but to the people here it is just like the crusades all over again. It's the same with the Sunni and the Shia. One minor disagreement about who was to follow Mohammed and everyone wants to kill each other. 'Has it always been like that here?' I asked, eager to learn more about the Professor's worldview and, in the process, to clarify mine.

'No. I came from the Kurdish north of the country and my childhood was very peaceful. It is very different up there. It is very green and in the years before Saddam it was like a paradise to live in.'

As I listened attentively to his story I realised that his life experience had enabled him to acknowledge the violence of the current conflict while believing passionately in a radiant vision of peace and prosperity for the future. As he spoke I was slowly gaining a deeper appreciation of his culture, his religion and the simple truths about his life. Everything he said was expressed with such upbeat candour and optimism, and what he told me made me realise that, despite all our apparent differences, we were in fact the same.

'Is it able to be fixed?'

'I don't know. It is bigger than both of us but it begins with us. If we can find peace within ourselves then we have a glimmer of hope that it will be seen by others and repeated.'

'Is it possible here?'

'A vicious cycle has been created here. It will not be easy.'

The vicious cycle to which the Professor alluded was something I'd begun to see and to understand for myself: an industry of violence and corruption resulting from the influx of US money into Iraq. The American dollar had overtaken the dinar as the currency of choice and the banking system had collapsed. With no credit or electronic facilities in the whole country, cash was king. Billions of dollars were flown in to help with the 'rebuilding' of the country, some of these funds being allocated to local police and military generals to pay their men. None of the payments was properly accounted for and many of the generals were taking a large percentage of the money for themselves instead of passing it on to their soldiers or policemen. But, even though they were being ripped off, these guys were at least fortunate enough to be employed, unlike many other Iraqis. Industry and commerce had ground to a halt with the invasion and had never recovered, so there were no jobs to be had, no way to make a living. Unable to sustain themselves in normal ways, many unemployed and poverty-stricken Iraqis had become part of the insurgency as a means to survive, not able to look beyond their immediate needs. It was almost as if they had no other choice.

'But it will have to start with men,' the Professor continued. 'Men have ruled here for so long and we have had war after war. Here we have a male-dominated culture, a culture in which men love to fight. Do you have the same?'

'Hang on, are you saying it's all men's fault?'

'No, but you must understand that most men are merely boys in adult bodies.'

'What does that mean?' I asked curiously.

'During childhood boys create a mask to show everyone else how they want to be seen. They learn this from their fathers or from the television. Have you not seen this?'

'Yes,' I said, thinking back to my own childhood.

'Some pretend to be tough, others pretend to be strong.'

'There are plenty of those here,' I said, interrupting him.

'Yes, and that is the problem. They are trying so hard to be the person they created many years before that they have lost the integrity to which I was referring.'

His observations definitely applied to me. Just as the Western media and the opinions of family and friends had conditioned me to fear the Muslim world and all it stands for, I had also grown up with a view of manhood that was dysfunctional. Believing that being a 'real' man depended upon mastering the essential elements of manhood—such as heterosexuality, aggression, courage and all-round blokiness—I had measured myself against these standards without even knowing it. Every argument I had with a boss or a spouse, every negative response I had to a difference of opinion, every hurt feeling I had when things didn't go my way and every disappointment I had felt when people hadn't met my personal expectations—all were a result of my cockeyed view of masculinity, driven by the unconscious fear I would be shamed if I didn't measure up.

I realised I had been fighting blind most of my life.

And I only had to look around to know I wasn't the only one. We were supposed to be in Iraq to help get the country back on its feet, but the blokes I worked with seemed to have other motives. They were driven by a need to prove themselves in some way or another, whether they knew it or not—and in most cases, not. It seemed the military/police culture was an attractive option for those who needed to prove who had the biggest dick.

'I'd never thought about it like that before,' I said, as the full significance of what he was saying washed over me.

'Not many do. But if men can find peace within themselves then we at least have a chance, and it will start with taming their ego.'

'Not getting rid of it as they teach in some cultures?'

'No, how can we get rid of something that is a part of us? It only needs to be controlled.'

His words cut deep. I'd fought for so long to control everything in my life—to be the master of every part of my domain and to be the master of every domain in which I found myself. Now, I realised I wasn't in control of my ego—it controlled me. The Professor was right. The only thing I could control was my attitude—and by approaching the world calmly and cultivating inner peace, I could improve my life and my relationships with others. If I could do that, hopefully others might recognise the change in me and follow suit, asking themselves the same questions I had.

'It's a bit like trying to walk a big dog that hasn't been trained,' I said with a laugh.

'What do you mean?'

'Well, from what you have told me, the untamed ego could be compared to a dog that drags its owner around the streets instead of walking calmly next to them as a companion.'

'Go on,' the Professor said, seemingly interested in my little allegory.

'If the dog is allowed to do whatever it wants, the owner becomes a slave to the dog's desire to sniff every tree and dog turd along the way.'

'And how does that relate to us?'

'If we let our ego run the show instead of the other way around, then we will always give in to our desires, even when it's to our detriment.'

'Yes,' said the Professor, now fully comprehending where I was coming from. 'Even to the point of going to war.'

Perhaps it was my time as a dog handler that led me to interpret the Professor's ideas in this way, but I began to think more about how dogs were like our own egos. Dogs are considered to be man's best friend and a dog that is loved and treated well will more than live up to this title, and so it is with the ego. Of course, there will be times when the dog will give in to its primal desires (after all, it is an animal) but this is not a time for punishment or trying to get rid of it by taking it to the pound. It is a time for understanding, humour and, if need be, discipline, so that the dog serves you instead of becoming a burden. There had, and would be, times when negative aspects of my masculine instincts would take over but instead of beating myself up about it I had to start to treat myself with understanding and compassion.

'How come we haven't spoken about all this before?' I asked the Professor, realising as I did that our previous conversations had been limited to his translator duties.

'Maybe you weren't ready to hear it.'

Perhaps it was because we were near Babylon, an ancient seat of wisdom and learning, or maybe it was just the heat, but as the impact of our conversation sunk deeper, I knew that beneath his guise as an interpreter for our company, the Professor was in fact a modern-day mystic, a teacher for the ages, arriving just when I was ready to accept his lessons.

20

Who's Driving the Bus?

Although I was a little unsure as to what would happen in the future I felt ready to undertake a long journey of self-discovery. I had needed to do this for some time, to finally let go, even if not entirely, of my old self. I was realistic enough to know that old habits die hard but I was up for the challenge. Self-examination and self-questioning had been a tradition in this part of the world for millennia and I felt it was now my turn. Jesus had apparently wandered in the desert to find himself. Mohammed did the same. Without intending to compare myself to these two great prophets, I felt I was embarking on a similar journey.

'Do you know the story of Captain Ahab?' the Professor asked.

'From *Moby Dick*?' I replied.

'Yes. Do you know it?'

'Not really. I know of the book but not what it's about.'

'That is a shame. It is a story which shows what we are talking about.'

'How so?'

'Captain Ahab was a man who was driven by revenge after losing his leg to Moby Dick. He was not able to see beyond his anger and it killed him in the end.'

It sounded like a book written about just about every guy I knew, including myself.

I began to think about the ways in which I was like Captain Ahab. How many times had I got myself into trouble by not wanting to back down? How many times had I not given up because I did not want to be seen as being weak, even if the outcome would be detrimental?

'I get where you're coming from,' I replied. 'I suppose it's just another example of how we can be driven by our ego if we're not paying attention.'

'Exactly! We must know when to quit instead of continuing on because we are worried about how we will look or whether we are right.'

'It's about balance isn't it?' I asked already knowing the answer.

'Yes, but it is not easy. Finding the right balance of ego and soul is tough but it is also the most important mission a man can undertake.'

'I know. I've made some huge mistakes in the past because I didn't know how to say "no" to myself.'

'And you will make more in the future, but hopefully over time you will learn to walk the fine line between being a hero and a coward. That is true courage.'

Like most people in Western society I was raised on Hollywood-style depictions of courage—of muscled heroes with immense moral fibre, impeccable manners and great abs fighting against adversity to save the day and get the girl (and all before breakfast). Think about Superman, Batman, Spiderman (or any of the other 'mans') and the pattern begins to emerge. Who wouldn't want to have a whole society of superheroes to look after the women and children, bravely holding the villain at bay with one hand while cradling a baby in the other—the perfect balance of Yin and Yang. The overuse of these images seems to have resulted in occupations like the police and military being seen as the exclusive domain of heroes. In fact these 'heroes' are just everyday people, going to work and doing what they've been trained to do, and the so-called courageous deeds they perform are an everyday part of their jobs—but that's not the way they are perceived in the wider community. I'd often seen the media coverage of incidents I'd been involved in, such as sieges, hostage rescues or counterterrorist operations, and the reports were so inaccurate that I sometimes found myself wondering: *was I at the same job?*

In a sad twist of irony, many injuries and deaths of emergency personnel around the world—including police, firefighters and soldiers—can be attributed to the pervasive need to maintain an image of competency and courage. In my opinion, too many guys die trying to be heroes.

Lost in my thoughts, I almost forgot that I was still involved in a conversation. I looked at the Professor and it dawned on me that he and I would soon be parting ways. The expats were scheduled to be deployed back to Baghdad the next day. I was a little disappointed. He'd helped me tap into my emotions in a way I'd never known and I wanted to be able to turn to him again if needed.

'What are you going to do when we leave here?' I asked.

'Whatever happens happens. I would like to teach again but we will see. Insha Allah.'

I'd heard the words 'insha Allah' many times since I'd been in Iraq. Simply translated as 'if God wills it', it was often used by our instructors or students if we asked them to do something. It was their way of saying 'I don't really want to but I'll do it anyway.' The Professor seemed to say it differently. He wasn't expressing resignation; instead he sounded relaxed, quietly confident that the cards would fall as they were meant to, almost as if everything was inevitable. Our path was laid out before us but what was to happen was also determined by the choices we made along that path. The words were so appropriate: paradoxical and yet perfect at the same time.

'If I don't see you before tomorrow, thank you.'

'Just remember, you are the one who is driving the bus,' he replied.

I looked at him quizzically, bemused by the odd reference.

'You are driving the bus,' he repeated. 'You are the one navigating through the streets of your life and I have simply climbed aboard and guided you through a part of the city with which you were not familiar—that is all.'

This guy was amazing, freely off-loading such amazing insights and wisdom without expecting anything in return.

'Thank you again. Salaam,' I said, placing my right hand across the middle of my chest.

He didn't reply. He just smiled and took another sip of his coffee, extending his hand in a gesture of cross-cultural understanding. I warmly shook it and nodded before turning and walking away.

The world somehow seemed completely different, as if I'd stepped from one realm and into another. My mind reeled. I knew I was rapidly approaching a crossroad and would have to make decisions from the heart and not the mind if I was to ensure my integrity remained intact. I had come to Iraq expecting to be challenged, but not like this. I had been jaded, looking for adrenaline and adventure to keep me interested and reaffirm my idea of who I was, and instead I found myself questioning my own identity and my deepest beliefs. Ironically, it was only amid the needless violence of a war zone that I had finally discovered my deep-seated desire for peace.

21

A Farewell to Arms

The day after my conversation with the Professor I gathered my kit and loaded it all back onto one of the Revas for the potentially dangerous two-hour drive back to the Green Zone. The company, having temporarily lost the training contract with the MOI, began to undertake the massive job of dismantling the infrastructure at the academy compound. Par for the company course, a skeleton crew was to stay behind and oversee its completion. I was more than a little glad I hadn't been asked to do the job.

All the weapons and ammunition stored in the armoury for distribution to graduating cadets had been packed into shipping containers and loaded onto the back of custom-fitted semitrailers; custom-fitted in that the outer shells of the truck doors were reinforced with heavy steel plating to give the driver some protection from small arms fire but, realistically, anything larger than an AK-47 round would pass through the added security like a hot knife through butter. Of more than five hundred contractor deaths since the coalition invasion (and by now I was sure it was indeed an invasion) the majority had been truck drivers, targeted for their load in much the same manner as stagecoaches robbed by bandits in the Wild West. Security concerns were obviously high, so those of us who were heading back to Baghdad for the long-awaited flight out of the country would be going along to provide a security convoy, ensuring that the weapons were transported safely back to the International Zone.

As the engines of the two Revas loudly roared into life I put on my body armour, Kevlar helmet and grabbed my AMD rifle and, for the first time, became aware of how false it felt to be wearing my gear. Physically I was protecting myself but emotionally I was merely putting my disguise back on. That no longer mattered, though— whatever mask I was wearing, I couldn't hide the changes happening inside. I looked around and saw Aahil and a couple of the other local instructors standing near the entrance. I walked over to him and he held out his hand, acknowledging our friendship. I knew I wouldn't see him again so I ignored his hand and embraced him instead.

'Thanks for everything, Aahil,' I said.

'No sweat, Horse,' he replied.

'We'll turn you into an Aussie yet!' I said, laughing. 'Do me a favour and take care of yourself,' I added.

Take care of yourself. I'd probably said it a thousand times as a throwaway comment but now I truly meant it.

'I will, Horse. Thank you.'

I said my farewells to the other instructors as well but by no means did I feel the same connection that I had with Aahil. Hopping into the back of the Reva, I watched him wave until the rear door closed and his face finally disappeared from view. I hoped he would some day experience the sort of peace and safety that people living in countries like Australia take for granted every day.

The rear of the Reva was cramped because of all the gear we had to transport back to the IZ, but luckily there were only three of us inside the cabin with another two manning the PKMs. AJ, the SAS trooper with whom I'd been on the roof during the incident at Camp Solidarity, was sitting next to me inside the cabin with Clint the 'boy watcher' sitting directly across from us.

'Hey, FOT,' AJ said.

'Yes, AJ?'

'It's easier if you leave the safety catch off your AMD. Just cock it, and if the shit hits the fan you're good to go.'

'Thanks, brother.'

I was glad he'd reminded me. In the event we were attacked and had to jump out of the APC, working the large cocking lever on the side of the weapon would be easier than trying to fiddle with the much smaller fire select lever. In many years of firearm instruction and operational experience I had learnt that it is better to rely on large muscle movements wherever possible—as in this example, working the cocking lever with the entire hand as opposed to manipulating the safety catch with the fingers. When you're under extreme duress, your heart rate is elevated beyond normal levels, and blood is pumped away from your extremities, making dextrous finger movements difficult to accomplish. I was hoping I wouldn't have to work the lever at all, though. I felt I had begun to find some clarity in my life and I couldn't wait to be out of Iraq. Try as I might, I couldn't shake the thought that it would be just my luck that in my last few hours in the country something would happen, and the new Horse would only be a short-lived entity.

Moving out of the front gates onto one of the arterial roads, it was obvious Clint hadn't heard AJ's words:

'Hey, Horse, your safety is off,' he said.

'I know.'

'Well it should be on. It's unsafe not to have it on.'

'It's not cocked.'

'Doesn't matter, company regulations say it should be on.'

I didn't even bother to reply. An uncocked weapon without a round in the chamber is about as deadly as a stick—you might as well try to hit someone with it because nothing dangerous is coming out the front. Looking at him with a 'shut the fuck up idiot or I'll rip your head off!' expression soon put an end to his questions. I actually did feel like ripping his head off, but I reminded myself of the previous day's conversation with the Professor. I took a moment to pay attention to what I was feeling, recognising I was probably a little nervous about the trip and was trying to make myself feel better by getting angry at Clint. It was my own fear causing the anger and if I didn't nip it in the bud it would escalate. I decided to let it go. I didn't need to prove anything to anyone.

My fears proved unfounded. The trip was uneventful and I passed the time listening to the dull drone of the engines, going over and over again in my mind the steps I would take if we were attacked. Peering out the windows at the landscape, distorted by the thickness of the armoured glass, I also pondered the life-changing incidents that had occurred while I was here and how they would shape my future.

Two hours and a sore arse later we came to a stop outside the company villa, where we'd be staying for the night before we flew home, back to the 'real' world. After we unloaded our gear, we ordered pizzas from the PX and washed them down with a few beers before settling in for our last night in Iraq. Standing on the roof of the villa, knocking back a beer and a cigarette, I looked out over the nightlights of the city, listening to the ever-present noise of the Blackhawk helicopters taking off and landing at Camp Washington, only a short distance away.

The next morning we ran the gauntlet along Route Irish to the Baghdad International Airport once more. When I took off the body armour and handed over the AMD I realised this was probably the last time I'd ever don any sort of tactical gear or handle a firearm. For the last decade, tactical gear had been like a protective exoskeleton but now I was relinquishing it, and when that weapon left my hand I felt an enormous sense of relief. These items were potent symbols of my former life and beliefs, but I was finally letting them go, releasing myself from their constricting grip. I felt reborn. A new chapter was about to begin. I did have conflicting emotions about leaving Iraq, though. On the one hand this place had been responsible for some serious personal growth, but on the other I was more than a little happy to be saying goodbye to the 'sandpit'.

With our weapons and gear offloaded we still had to go through three very rigid security checks before we were allowed to enter the departures lounge. Once through we headed to the gate to wait for our plane back to Dubai, finding a space on the floor to stretch out and relax. With nothing else to do I looked around and saw a lot of people in this area of the terminal; far too many it seemed for the flight.

'What's with all the people?' I asked one of the boys who'd been through the process before.

'They sell more tickets than there are seats, just in case.'

'Just in case of what?'

'In case some people can't get here for security reasons. We just have to make sure we're at the front of the line.'

The bloke wasn't wrong either.

When the announcement came (three hours late) that the flight was open for boarding there was no semblance of what could be called a line. Everybody, including a number of Iraqi men, women and children were pushing their way forward, desperate to make sure they got a seat. I couldn't really blame them; for all I knew securing a seat on this flight could have been their only hope of escape. There was no way I could begrudge them a little pushing and shoving.

After handing out and receiving more than a few swinging elbows in the surging crowd, I made my way onto the exact same piece of shit aircraft I arrived in. Making sure to choose a seat that was bolted to the floor this time, I settled back and tried to relax, confident that the flight out would be more comfortable. The plane climbed rapidly rather than spiralling like a corkscrew, making for the safety of altitude to avoid the chance of surface-to-air missiles before heading south-east toward Dubai. As I looked out the window at the desert landscape below I thought about the huge mess we were leaving behind. I'd come here to help, to put things back in order, but I hadn't understood the scale of the devastation the invasion had wrought on Iraq. Mopping up would be a massive task, and it would take many, many years.

Having realised at last that I'd been wearing a mask all my life, I suddenly found myself thinking about masks on a larger scale, and how the governments of the world disguise their true intentions with empty political rhetoric. Bringing democracy and freedom to Iraq was merely an excuse; in truth the world's leaders were seeking to prove their dominance through violence and intimidation. It was about their collective ego, not their desire to help the Iraqi people.

Deciding I'd done enough thinking for one day I settled back into my seat and drifted into a sound sleep even before we reached our cruising altitude of 30,000 feet.

22

The Hills Are Alive...

Part of our employment contract meant we were supplied with return tickets to Australia. I was due to fly out of Dubai the day after returning from Iraq but I felt an irresistible urge to experience more of what the world had to offer. Indefinitely deferring my return, I booked a flight to Athens that would become the starting point for a European escapade—I was happy to go where the wind took me, no plans, no agendas.

As the Professor and other Iraqis would say: insha Allah. I was going wherever God willed it.

I'd found a deeper appreciation of life in the desert but I needed time to take things in and think them over. While I hadn't spent a huge amount of time in Iraq it still felt like I'd stepped into a parallel realm where the rules of the real world did not apply, and I wasn't sure how I'd settle back into normal life. For the past decade or more, my life had been completely regimented and structured: every single move leading towards some higher goal and higher purpose. I'd spent so much time trying to make myself into something I wasn't, something false. I knew I had to take stock. I had to work out who I actually was— and unplanned and unstructured travel seemed the perfect way to start.

Athens ended up becoming a mere stepping stone to the Greek island of Santorini, a beautiful, though sparsely vegetated, extinct volcano that served as the perfect place to acclimatise back into civilisation. Spending a week drinking cocktails by the beach and soaking in the relaxed lifestyle was the perfect antidote to everything I'd known for the past few months. With my head becoming a little clearer I decided it was time to head back to the hustle and bustle of Athens. I whipped around the city and took in many of the sights. My time in Iraq had rekindled my interest in history and Athens was the perfect place to continue my learning. Walking around the Acropolis and Agora added to my growing awareness of just how small and insignificant we really are. These monuments to human ingenuity had been here for thousands of years and would probably still be here long after I was dead and gone. It hit home hard, making me see that I was but one small cog in the broader mechanism.

I eventually found myself in an internet cafe. Caution thrown to the wind, I decided my next destination would be dictated by the cheapest flight leaving Athens the following day. I didn't want to ponder the question even for a second. My life had been so regimented and I'd been so accustomed to making long-term decisions—now I just wanted to do things on the spur of the moment and I was revelling in making snap decisions. Whether it was travelling on a bus, a flight or a train, making decisions on the spur of the moment was rather therapeutic.

The cheapest flight took me to an airfield that was once the mainstay of air traffic movement within the old East German regime, Schönefeld Airport in Berlin. Standing in the non–European Union line I was beckoned toward an exit gate by a stern-looking German customs official. I half-expected he would ask to see my papers but he seemed to be more interested in reducing the line out of the terminal than checking passports—comically different to the Communist border guards I'd seen in early eighties movies. Walking out through the turnstiles with my passport unchecked and unstamped, I collected my bags and headed into the city proper, ending up at a funky-looking backpacker joint.

The next day I set out on a walking tour around a city that, like Baghdad, had seen more than its fair share of horror and spawned one of the world's best known and cruellest dictators. Something else struck me about Berlin. It came across as a city of immense contrast. It had been the focal point of Allied attacks during World War II and a seemingly endless barrage of bombs had all but destroyed the city's infrastructure and historic buildings, but it still seemed to ooze a charm that belied its history. The more I immersed myself in the city the more I gained a sense of what can only be described as a rebellion against authority, a freedom from the oppression that had dominated German culture for much of the twentieth century.

This feeling was something to which I could totally relate. Part of me had been beholden to a dictator and an authoritarian system: my ego. Berlin had its own experience with dispelling the demons of a dictatorship and therefore, I reasoned, it was the ideal place for me to do the same.

I took in all the popular tourist sights: the Brandenburg Gate, the Reichstag and Checkpoint Charlie. While they were awesome to see it was a small memorial to an incident on the night of 10 May 1933 that stood out for me. The Bebelplatz is a public square right in the middle of the city housing a memorial to the infamous book burning event that occurred as part of the systematic destruction of material deemed to be a threat to the Nazi ideology. Some forty thousand books were burned that night in a frenzy of nationalistic pride by students and hardline party members, all swept along by the Nazi propaganda machine. The burnt books were symbolised by empty shelves in an underground chamber, viewed through a heavy glass panel.

Standing in the square looking down at the empty shelves below my feet, I thought about the act of madness that had taken place over seventy years earlier. It was so long ago, and yet the mentality that led to the events of that night is still very much a part of the modern psyche.

People don't burn books openly anymore, at least not that I know of, but we still have an us-versus-them mentality: 'If you're not with us, you're against us.' This had been my attitude, and that was how I'd ended up in Iraq, 'doing my bit for my country'. When I first arrived there, I had genuinely believed that all Muslims were terrorists, my understanding of the conflict shaped by the Western media. My contact with the people there had shown me I was wrong.

The most convenient and effective method of delivering the message of superiority over other cultures, races or countries, it struck me, is through the mechanism of blind patriotism. Hitler used it. So did Saddam. But sadly it is not just a tool used by despots to have others do their bidding. It is extremely popular in so-called modern-thinking Western societies, albeit disguised behind loin-stirring patriotic rhetoric.

Thinking about the events of that night in 1933 put everything into perspective. I could not judge any actions as being good or bad; the truth was just too blurred. Things were as they were.

Something told me my time in Berlin was done; its lessons had been imparted and I needed a new adventure. I went to the Hauptbahnhof, Berlin's new main railway station, which had only opened a few months earlier. It was a space-age multi-level railway hub sporting a massive Departures/Arrivals board, like those found in international airports. I considered my options.

Where *did* I want to go next?

Having no real game plan, I decided to stick to my original strategy and take the next cheap train out of the country no matter where it might be headed.

It was Prague.

As good a place as any, I thought, handing over the thirty euro for the ticket. An hour later the train departed and I settled into a comfortable seat for the five-hour trip through south-eastern Germany then on to Prague. About three hours into the journey two border guards, one German, the other Czech, walked through the carriage.

'Your passport, please?' the German guard asked me in perfect English.

I handed it to her thinking, *this is more like how I've seen it in the movies.*

'You do not have a stamp in here for Germany.'

Oh, shit! I thought when I remembered I'd been ushered through the EU line on my arrival.

'I didn't get one when I arrived.'

'How did you get here?'

'I flew into Schönefeld two days ago and they didn't give me a stamp.'

I looked at her as she processed what I'd said, trying to read her body language to see if I truly was busted or not. After about thirty seconds of deliberation she looked at me and handed back my passport.

'Okay, enjoy your trip to the Czech Republic.'

'Thank you,' I said, smiling back at her.

So much for the movies, I thought, relaxing back into my seat.

Prague was a pleasant enough place but I wanted more from my experience than just looking at old buildings. As much as I appreciated the architecture and the immense history places like Prague afforded, I started to think that

I'd become a little like Chevy Chase's character, Clark Griswold, in *European Vacation*.

'Hey look kids . . . Big Ben, Parliament,' I said to myself every time I saw a new old building. Serious travellers may not forgive me for saying this, but apart from a bicycle ride around the city, I got bored fairly quickly. On a whim, I boarded a bus to Vienna.

After a brief one-night stopover in Vienna I found myself in the Austrian city of Salzburg. Unlike the previous cities, all of which gave me something to ponder as I learned more about other history and cultures, Salzburg made me stop and think about my macho image as the stereotypical 'man's man'. A beautifully serene city, Salzburg was where *The Sound of Music* was filmed. I'd been a fan of the famous musical since I was a child so I took the opportunity to go on a tour.

It was a surreal experience. Walking onto the bus I stood out immediately. Here I was single and *straight*. All the other blokes were either overtly gay or obviously married. The married ones, from the pained expressions on their faces, were none too pleased (but didn't want to show it) about being dragged along by their wives. As the tour progressed, most of us (except for a few of the husbands) sang along to tunes from the movie. I had to laugh at myself. How would I tell people back home that someone like me went on the SOM tour by myself and, not only that, had a great time. Near the end I started talking to a girl from Melbourne who was travelling with a gay male friend.

'What are you doing on the tour?' she asked.

'Why do you ask?' I responded with a huge smile on my face.

'You don't seem to fit the profile of guys who would like *The Sound of Music*.'

'Ah, well, stereotypes are meant to be broken,' I said cheekily.

Happy with our new-found acquaintance the three of us organised to go for dinner and a drink at a beer hall overlooking the city at the end of the tour. Over our meal we chatted a bit more and exchanged personal stories about where we were from and where we were going, and I told them about some of my experiences in Iraq.

'So you've just been to Iraq and now you're here on a Sound of Music tour?' the girl said, a little perplexed.

'You're a bit like Shrek. Many deep layers . . . like an onion,' her friend added.

I loved the comparison and laughed heartily. The beer continued to flow and so did the laughs. I was grateful to be able to do something I really enjoyed without worrying what someone else might think. Liberating, that's what it was. I felt far freer and far happier than I ever remembered being.

Continuing my cultural sojourn across Europe I headed down to Rome and then up through Florence, Pisa and across to the French Riviera city of Nice, taking in many wonderful sights and districts such as Tuscany and Monaco along the way. In Nice I hired a car and drove up through the middle of France. Believing what others had said, I'd blindly accepted that French people were rude and intolerant of visitors. However, my experience could not have been further from this. I experienced warmth and gratitude at every stop and it was this gracious manner that endeared the countryside, and its people, to me.

France held a deeper interest for me because ever since I was a young boy I'd had a passion for military history, which probably explains my career choices. I'd often read about the major battle sites in France and seen photos and documentaries about them. Two places of particular interest to me were Normandy and the Somme.

Sitting on the sea wall at Omaha beach, Normandy, I looked out over a huge expanse of coastline and could feel the history in the air. I was *actually* at the place where the Allied forces finally gained a foothold on European soil against the occupying German army in June 1944. I gazed out over the landscape and thought about how this related to my life. Those few hundred yards of beach were like my decades of chasing the macho dream—flat and without form. After years of war within myself I was embarking on a reclamation of territory.

Staring out across the sand I could only imagine the terror the soldiers would have experienced knowing they had to traverse a wide, well-defended beach adjacent to the sea wall, the famous MG-42 machine guns spewing up to 1500 rounds per minute towards them as they advanced. I'd seen this weapon in action when I was in Iraq. One of the boys acquired one from somewhere (I didn't ask!) and we took it down onto the range for a test fire. I am by no means a gun nut but the rate at which this weapon delivered its deathly payload was something to behold and I could totally understand why the Allied soldiers held such a healthy respect for its capabilities. I mean, I'd been shot at when I was in special operations but it was nothing like what must have occurred here. Thankfully, I had not been involved in direct conflict in Iraq, but the experience itself was enough to highlight the pointlessness of human conflict. I couldn't think of a better example than where I now sat. It was a bleak illustration of the futile, ridiculous nature of war. The sense of waste was only amplified as I walked through the US cemetery near the small town of Colleville-sur-Mer. My thinking was clearer now than it had been in a long time, and the destructive nature of the driven male ego became painfully apparent. War was just an exaggerated version of young boys jockeying in the schoolyard for the position of top dog.

I began to gain more of an appreciation of the idea of dying for one's country and one's beliefs. Human beings have been fighting wars for generations and yet we're still fighting them. Society hasn't learned anything from all this tragic loss of life. Young men and women are still dying at somebody else's say so.

Patriotism has a lot to answer for, I thought as I wandered among the pristine white crosses dotting the landscape.

The next day I drove back through the hedgerows lining the lush green farming fields of Normandy on my way to the small northern town of Villers-Bretonneux.

If the senseless waste of human life that was warfare hadn't hit home at Normandy it certainly did when I arrived at the Western Front. It astounded me that two armies had built a continuous trench line from

Switzerland to the North Sea—the equivalent of a trench running from Sydney to Melbourne—and I couldn't help marvelling at what humans can achieve. Mostly, though, I was disappointed to think that we use these impressive skills and capabilities to kill each other. As I made my way around the Western Front I was amazed to learn that the River Somme was the site of the British Army's heaviest losses in a single day. On 16 July 1916, the British general Douglas Haig devised a plan whereby they would shell the German lines for days on end. Something like one million shells were sent over. Thinking the German lines must have been destroyed, the English sent their guys over at a walk—a sensible plan on paper except for the fact that the Germans had deep dugouts into which they retreated when the shelling started. Once it had stopped they clambered back out and readied themselves for the inevitable assault. The Allied guys simply walked into a firestorm of machine-gun fire. They didn't stand a chance.

Sixty thousand casualties in one day! What a waste.

Now, here's the real kicker: the English and German royal families are related! So, while there was obviously more to it, with things like colonialism and jostling for empire, et cetera, what the war boiled down to was nothing more than a large family squabble, with the average Joe paying the price.

Wandering around the now green fields, it was difficult to imagine what this place must have looked like during the First World War. All I'd seen pictures of was barren and desolate landscapes, all but stripped of any semblance of life. When I eventually came across an abandoned

English trench, I stood where the parapets would have been and looked up the hill towards the German lines. I tried to imagine the hail of gunfire, remembering how I felt when I fired an M16 for the first time, the sense of finality as I realised how easily these weapons killed. It was so different to what I'd seen on TV or imagined when playing war games as a child. Multiply that feeling by a few thousand and that's what would have greeted the soldiers from both sides as they made their way through the mud and bodies to attack a position they had little chance of taking. My doubts about patriotism only heightened as I tried to think what must have been going through their minds just before they went over the top. I tried to put myself in their shoes. I wondered whether I could do it, jumping out of a trench and running towards heavily fortified machine-gun posts knowing with certainty I was going to be killed or wounded.

My time was beginning to run short and I desperately wanted to see Paris so I left the Western Front. Driving back toward the French capital on a warm summer's evening I was excited to be visiting this most famous of cities, and my anticipation built as I navigated carefully through its outer suburbs. As I finally approached the city centre I was awestruck by its radiance: it really is the 'city of lights'. I was apprehensive about driving in such a huge metropolis, especially on a different side of the road, but I actually found it quite easy to do as long as I didn't try to look at all the sights at the same time. The Parisian drivers were very forgiving as I manoeuvred my way around the Arc de Triomphe, the Champs-Élysées and the Place de la

Concorde. It was so different to driving in Sydney, where most people are too arrogant and impatient to allow other cars to merge and blend peacefully. If you took a bird's eye view of Paris's main streets it would look absolutely chaotic, but the courteous and obliging Parisians seemed to embrace the road rules as guidelines only, allowing cars to merge and flow in a daily dance that ensured tempers did not get frayed.

Staying in the Montmartre district in the north of the city, a famous base for many of the world's greatest artists such as Vincent Van Gogh, Pablo Picasso and Claude Monet, I was determined to get around and see as much as I could. Driving in Paris was fun, but I was beginning to feel that I was missing a lot of the nitty-gritty of the city so I hired a bike and set out on my own magical mystery tour. Seeing the sights like the Eiffel Tower, the Louvre and Notre Dame was, of course, an amazing experience but none of these provided my greatest pleasure. Instead, it was the simple act of sitting at a sidewalk cafe on a busy boulevard near the Sacré-Cœur Basilica, relaxing over a coffee as I watched the world go by.

All too soon it was time to head to the airport for the flight back to Dubai and then home. Similar to most major airports around the world, Paris's Charles de Gaulle international gateway was a hive of activity, especially in the security-conscious aftermath of the 9/11 attacks—and the line for the security baggage checkpoint was huge.

Lucky I'm early, I thought. When I reached the customs control point, the immaculately dressed customs officer looked through the myriad stamps in my passport.

His official demeanour remained until he came across something that sparked his interest and a curious look came over his face.

'You have been to Iraq?' he questioned as he looked up from my passport at me.

'Yes.'

'Come with me.'

I didn't know what to expect. Perhaps there was a security problem with people who had been to Iraq, or maybe this was somehow linked to the French government's refusal to participate in the coalition invasion. As I walked behind the customs officer I smiled as I remembered something a US soldier had told me about France not helping with the 'problem' in the Middle East: 'Going to war without the French is like bear hunting without a piano accordion . . . you don't need 'em.'

Thoughts about being taken into a small office and asked a thousand questions ran through my head. I hoped they wouldn't take too long and I wouldn't miss my flight. Then an even nastier thought occurred to me. In a lawless country like Iraq, drugs were a big problem, and I began to wonder about the true extent of the smuggling. As we moved further and further along the queue I was sure I was in for a full cavity search and I certainly wasn't relishing the thought of someone's gloved hand probing my nether regions.

I needn't have worried.

The customs officer took me to the front of the queue and indicated that I should put my bags on the scanner conveyor and walk through.

It was as if he felt obliged to give me special treatment because of a stamp in my passport. Realising quickly what had happened I turned to him.

'*Merci*,' I said in my best French accent.

'You are welcome. Enjoy your flight,' he replied.

An hour later I was on the plane back to Dubai for a one-night stopover before heading back home.

Boarding the Emirates A-340 Airbus the next day for the fifteen-hour flight back to Sydney I felt a sense of both an ending and a beginning. My seven-week sojourn around Europe had been a great escape and, enjoying every moment, I'd not given much thought to the fact that the day would come when I had to return to the real world. Amidst the beers and sightseeing (as well as a few show tunes on the SOM tour) I'd unconsciously delayed thinking about what I would do when I got home. Apart from seeing my long-suffering children, whose father had been absent in body and mind for a number of years, I'd be making it up as I went along—much like the trip I had just undertaken. Settling into the economy-class seat for the long flight home I was both excited and a little scared. As the flight made its way across the Indian Ocean toward familiar shores I closed my eyes and drifted off to sleep as the questions continued to scroll through my mind— questions I hoped would some day be answered.

It was the first day of spring when the A-340 touched down at Sydney Airport and after clearing customs I was elated to see my two children, Alex and Jessica, waiting for me when I came out into the arrivals lounge. Seeing them for the first time in many months was overwhelming and I shed more than a few tears as I wholeheartedly embraced them. Nicole had brought them to see me arrive and I was grateful our once rocky relationship following our divorce was showing significant signs of improvement. She looked happy and I was happy for her. She'd recently met and become engaged to a bloke who seemed to care deeply for her, and for the children, and I was truly thankful. Regardless of the past, she was now able to move forward and make a life with her husband-to-be and the children, a circumstance that was best for everyone.

23

Number Elevens

In the months following my return to Australia my life seemed to be spiralling out of control, almost like the plane that had delivered me into Baghdad over a year before. I was wallowing in uncertainty, wrestling with who I now was. All my adult life I'd been trying to prove how tough I was—it was how I defined myself, the source of my identity. While I was in Europe I felt I could be whoever I wanted to be; I didn't have to prove myself anymore. Dropping the macho swagger was bliss, like the sensation of lightness I'd felt when I taken off my sand-filled backpack on the selection course a few years earlier. But when I returned home, even though I knew I'd disposed of the former me . . . it left a vacuum.

I was completely, utterly, totally and hopelessly lost. Catching up with old workmates for a beer was difficult because I couldn't relate to their view of the world, despite sharing the same ideas only months before. Chatting to women in a pub or a club meant fighting the temptation to portray myself as a hero in order to score points. I was neither here nor there. All I knew was that I was in an extremely uncomfortable place and it was totally foreign to me.

I'd always made sure not to let anyone get too close, never really showing anyone my feelings. Not when my marriage broke down. Not in any of the several short relationships that followed. Not even when my children begged me to pay attention to them when they were hurt or upset. Looking back I was only living half a life, not for a moment realising there was a better way. I was dejected and unhappy to the point of feeling numb, unable to sleep without the assistance of pills or alcohol. I had difficulty concentrating and began to lose weight as an endless stream of negative thoughts scrolled through my head. If I didn't continue my life as a so-called tough guy, who was I going to be? Would my whole world begin to crumble around me if I let my guard down? Would people still respect me? Everywhere I looked it was the macho men who people seemed to look up to—or did they?

I was glued to the couch watching the TV and seeing image after image of what it supposedly meant to be a 'real man'. I needed to find a new job, or at least something to keep me occupied, but I had always done police work and found it hard to think of other options. The worst part was that the longer I sat there the more I thought. There were so many things I wanted to do with my life, but I just couldn't nail what they might be. So many times I contemplated how easy it would be to go back to what I knew, surrounding myself with familiar workmates in familiar work situations, but that would make it so much harder to escape the trap I'd made for myself. Slowly I began to realise that, by holding everything close and never talking about what really mattered, I'd been living a lie. I was terrified of showing my true self, of being authentic. Since childhood I'd been imbued (as we all are) with the Australian sense of manhood—through stories of soldiers in wartime, images on the TV screen and lessons from older generations. I didn't feel it was the done thing to open up and express emotions because I thought it made me vulnerable. But then I realised the opposite was true.

I looked at the way I'd been living and realised that the pressure of covering up reality was overwhelming. I knew I couldn't go on like this. It was too hard. It didn't make me feel good about who I was. I had all the trappings of success, but felt empty inside.

Sitting alone one night watching TV, I started to cry; not just a few tears but uncontrollable sobbing. This shook me to the core, because guys don't cry, or at least that's what I'd grown up to believe—but real guys do cry. Real guys are not afraid of showing they're human. If someone had told me a few years ago that men can cry I would have laughed at them or perhaps made fun of them. I suppose I just had to find out the hard way. I cried for a good half-hour, only stopping when I'd released the build-up of anguish and frustration. I had no idea how much I'd been holding in all those years, how much I'd kept from those I loved because I was so caught up in appearances. I wept and wept, unable to control the 'number elevens'—a slang term for the two lines of snot that run out of your nose after contact with tear gas. It felt painful and exhilarating at the same time. I kept thinking to myself: *You are not your job . . . you are not your job.*

The funny thing was that even when I was in the middle of my super-charged macho life in tactical operations, deep down I knew the image I projected to my mates, to everyone I cared about, was a fraud. After a hostage rescue operation in Wollongong one day in 2004 I was walking back down the street toward our equipment truck wearing the full gamut of tactical equipment with a swagger that would make Rambo proud. A group of residents had gathered to watch the proceedings and, as I walked past, I overheard one of them say, 'Geez . . . I wouldn't want to mess with that guy.'

Before I had a chance to react accordingly, maybe throwing in a bit more swagger or even a stern 'don't fuck with me' look, the real me spoke up, surprising me: *If he only knew how much of a softy I really am.*

I began to realise the tough guy stuff was a way of covering up all the pain I'd ever felt. It was a little bit like the pain a kid feels when he's snubbed in the schoolyard by his mates or by the girl in his class who thinks he isn't worthy of her attention. It was like the pain when you feel your parents aren't giving you enough attention or when you believe that nobody likes you. As a kid I would always pretend not to care but it really hurt like hell. Whether the pain was real or imagined, I carried this tactic of dealing with it into adulthood, building my very own Berlin Wall as protection: not letting anyone or anything in and not letting much out either.

For all the things that I'd done that were considered tough this was the hardest. I'd endured numerous life-threatening situations in the adrenaline-driven world of counterterrorism and Special Ops, but now I felt scared and exposed in a way I'd never experienced before. That's why I think guys don't bother—they take what seems like the easy route. But the problem is that the pain just keeps on building, until it becomes unbearable. That's when guys top themselves, or lose themselves in alcohol, in recreational drugs, or in serial relationships that go nowhere. It's life on the run, never stopping long enough to ask the big questions: Who am I really? What do I want from life?

I discovered that when you don't ask the big questions, nothing changes. You don't progress. When I *finally* started to ask myself the questions I desperately needed to, I began to realise that this impenetrable barrier I'd built up acted as a shield against all the psychological trauma I'd experienced at work. You can't watch people die in car accidents or pick up body pieces after an explosion without it affecting you in some way. What doesn't help is when you're all pretending everything's cool when, truthfully, it's not. Like all the other guys, I gave the impression nothing ever really got to me. Thinking back, it was absolute insanity. But that's what guys do to each other—we keep silent about the stuff that's really important and stop others from talking about it too, by mocking them or taunting them or worse, because talking about our emotions would jeopardise our positions within the group. That's what happens when you haven't matured inside. You're still a sixteen-year-old kid, too scared to be real; still protecting yourself from rejection in the schoolyard. I know that's what the barbs from my fellow operatives were all about and I did everything I could to reinforce the tough guy image as well.

A few weeks after the seemingly endless sobbing subsided I went with some friends to a yum cha restaurant in Chatswood for some lunch. I was the only single guy in the group and we joked about relationships and life in general. In between the barbecue pork buns and the deep-fried chicken dumplings, Cathy, a psychologist friend of mine, said, 'You must have been involved in some very violent situations.'

'I suppose so,' I said matter-of-factly.

'What like?'

'Heaps of stuff, I suppose,' I responded, trying to deflect her questions.

'Are there any in particular that stand out?' she pressed.

I finally relented.

'I think my most vivid memory is of seeing a teenage boy ending his life by shooting himself in the head with a shotgun. Why?'

She looked at me quizzically.

'Did that affect you?'

'I don't think so,' I said, not really sure if it had or if it hadn't.

'Okay. Well, if it didn't affect you, what about your relationships?'

It was then I realised the exact line of her questions. Cathy wasn't probing for stories out of morbid curiosity. She was gently trying to point out the effect that my total detachment from these experiences had on my personal life. In many ways I had been an emotionless robot. When I went home at the end of the working day the force field was still up, causing a rift between me and everyone else. I hadn't realised till now how this contributed to a breakdown in relationships with my wife and others.

'Should we find a couch somewhere?' I said, laughing nervously, trying my best to avoid giving Cathy an answer.

'No, this isn't a session—I'm just curious about how people in that line of work deal with the trauma.'

'To be honest, I hadn't really thought about it.'

'So how did you deal with it?'

'I didn't. I just swept it under the carpet like most people, I think.'

Her line of questioning began to open my eyes. I realised that for police officers, and other people in high-pressure jobs, this shutting-down happened a lot. I'd seen it on many occasions. People I worked with over the years were right beside me but I never understood what effect our job had on them, let alone on myself. Sadly, a couple of former colleagues had committed suicide and I never really took the time to ask myself why, simply putting it down to an inability to deal with trauma. From what I have seen, my method of dealing with traumatic experiences was what guys tend to do all over the world. These experiences get shut out and forgotten about until they come later back to bite us on the arse, usually in the form of uncontrollable anger or grief. I saw plenty of guys absolutely lose the plot over seemingly minor things because the pressure of not expressing their emotions had reached boiling point and no-one ever told them there was another way. I'd also seen how my ex-wife, Nicole, had been deeply affected by incidents soon after the fact, and it was completely different. She was able to process the trauma, express the emotion and let it go—it didn't become a ticking time bomb.

'Is ignoring the problem more common among guys?' Cathy asked, apparently reading my thoughts.

'Come again?'

'Have you seen it more in men than in women?'

'Yes, I think men like to look like we're in control,' I told her.

I thought back to what the Professor had said about the 'essential' elements of manhood, such as aggression and courage, and how they can cloud our judgement, making us fight blindly against things without knowing why.

I was thankful for the short conversation with Cathy. It had sparked something in me—another 'light bulb' moment—and it would help me take one more step toward becoming a more balanced guy, just like my talk with the Professor had months earlier. It had been very confronting, but liberating too.

We finished our meal and I headed back home. I drove in silence, my thoughts transfixed on what lay ahead. I began to realise something special was going on. I was at the crossroads, but it needn't be a bad thing. I could continue to be defensive, or I could take note of every chance meeting or encounter I had with someone who made me think about where I wanted to be. These moments were invaluable; they helped me to take stock. After daring to look at where I'd been, I was now able to focus on where I was going. It was going to be a long and sometimes bumpy road, but I also knew it was time to move on and get a life.

24

Gentle Strength

As a guy who was used to getting his own way, I wanted the changes I was making to myself to be done and dusted so I could move on, but it was hard to break out of old patterns. I soon found myself falling back into my familiar ways, drinking heavily and going out clubbing, the same old same old. I was looking for a quick fix and, desperate for relief from my pain, I again sought the solace of short-term relationships.

Instead of seeking any deeper connection, once again I went for the glitz and glamour, turning my attentions toward a gorgeous, olive-skinned brunette with a fantastic body who seemed to fit all my criteria. Looking back, she was a predictable choice. Her physical appearance and mannerisms were remarkably similar to those of many girls I'd been with in the past. This new relationship was like the one I'd had with Sasha a few years earlier: a great physical attraction, but nothing deeper, nothing that was likely to make us last. I'd chosen another woman who reinforced my image of myself—how I *thought* I was, and how I wanted to be seen by others.

Within a month or so our relationship hit rock bottom. Once more my poor choice of partner came back to bite, harder than ever, and with it came the familiar feeling of abandonment and low self-worth. It's a bad space to be in.

After the break-up I went out for a few drinks one night with a bloke called Craig, a good mate who I'd met at an engagement party while working with his brother-in-law at Special Ops. We hit it off immediately and in the years after we often laughed about how I no longer kept in touch with his brother-in-law, preferring the company of someone who didn't work at the unit.

On this particular night Craig and I visited many hotels and proceeded to get well and truly rotten drunk. Usually when I was drinking I liked to maintain some sort of control, always aware of the dangers of getting too pissed—after all I'd seen hundreds if not thousands of people who'd gone past the point of no return and regretted it later. But this occasion was not one of them. As a good mate, Craig could see what was happening. He knew I'd gone through another painful, failed short-term relationship, and he also knew of my desire to move away from my previous vocation and the world I'd been living in. After way too many drinks Craig and I got into a taxi and headed to his house, where I was going to stay the night.

'Are you all right, Horsey?' he asked.

I didn't answer.

Almost comatose, I slumped into the taxi for the thirty-minute cab ride home. Once we got to Craig's place we sat on the lounge and I put my head into my hands in quiet desperation. Not knowing what to say or do Craig suggested the next best thing.

'Kick your shoes off, Horsey . . . you'll feel heaps better.'

Even in my wretched state I couldn't help but laugh at the ridiculousness of his statement but, not being one to resist the temptation of feeling better, I did what he suggested. I kicked off my shoes and leant back into the soft lounge; it did provide some relief.

What was going on? Was this my midlife crisis?

If it was, wasn't I supposed to rush out and buy a red sports car complete with the standard issue blonde in the passenger seat?

Not likely. I don't like red cars and I prefer brunettes.

I still didn't fully comprehend that I was setting myself up for this pain and disappointment by basing my relationship choices on physical attraction. I had grown and changed so much—but it wasn't enough. I wasn't putting what I'd learned into practice. I'd talked the talk without walking the walk—and so I still made it my priority to find the most attractive girls to go out with. Why do blokes do this when deep down we know it's likely to end in tears? I'm not alone in this type of fruitless pursuit and nor am I the first to be trapped by it. Society's obsession with beauty is as long as history itself.

Think of the story of the sirens from ancient Greek mythology, who lured sailors to their deaths with their seductive song. The beautiful images the women's voices conjured in the sailors' minds far outweighed the consequences they knew they would face if they gave in to their urges. True or not, this cautionary tale has stood the test of time for good reason. We just keep repeating the same errors.

I continued to date women who would make me look good in front of others, rather than women who would make me happy, still blinded by the idea that my worth as a man was somehow based on how hot my dates were. In the Professor's terms, I was letting my ego drive my decisions about relationships, rather than being guided by my soul.

I know now that by going out with attractive women I was trying to make myself look powerful and cover up feelings of insecurity. I didn't want to be seen as weak, and I felt vulnerable being alone. To maintain the upper hand in my relationships, I was often manipulative or secretive. If I didn't feel that I was good enough for my current girlfriend, that I was 'punching above my weight', as I'd often been told when I was with Sasha, I would cheat on her. I thought that gave me power, but it inevitably led to a break-up, leaving me alone and feeling vulnerable again. I was on a treadmill that was getting faster and faster, doing everything I could to keep up but rapidly running out of breath.

I did sometimes go out with girls who didn't fit all my preconceived ideas about the perfect partner, but after a short fling, they were discarded without any real explanation. It became such a pattern that once, after I'd been out on a couple of dates, my flatmate asked me whether I'd given this latest filly 'the talk'. The talk was pretty simple, an extended version of the age-old 'it's not you, it's me', which I used many times as a means of escape. During one of these short flings a girl I had been seeing told me she bought a copy of *He's Just Not That Into You*, a book about how and why men don't want to commit in relationships; it was a sure-fire signal she knew I wasn't really in it for the long haul. As each of these experiences came and went the feeling of loneliness settled like a thick fog. It somehow seemed worst when I was the one who didn't want to take it any further.

There was no real crisis point, just a growing consciousness that I needed to make a change. When I thought back to my conversations with the Professor I could now see that by not living within my integrity, by letting my ego run the show, I could never be whole nor happy. If I allowed my ego to feed my fear of being alone, weak or hurt, it would forever be the master and I would forever be the servant.

The time had come to take control and it needed to start with understanding the most primal of male urges: sex.

I mean let's get clear on this; men love sex.

It is a pleasurable and powerful driving force and certainly worthy of note—people have written songs, sonnets, poems and stories about the positive side of sex for as long as the human race has existed—but there's more to it than that. Sexual success has long been portrayed as the benchmark of manhood. The perception is that every 'conquest' contributes to a man's status and power, building his sense of self at the same time that it builds him up in the eyes of others. A 'real man' should be getting lots of sex.

I know from experience, though, that pursuing sex for the sole goal of getting your rocks off is folly. Funnily enough, when I was in my strongest physical shape, fully immersed in the game of chasing the opposite sex, I was at my weakest mentally. I put all of my energies into maintaining my image and although I was constantly playing this game of hide the sausage I recognise now that I was doing so out of an intense neediness.

I made a conscious decision to get off the treadmill so I could concentrate on understanding what I really wanted from a relationship. This resulted in abstinence from any sexual or intimate contact for over three years! I have no doubt many men would wince at this thought and see it as a complete undermining of their masculinity, but I saw it as an achievement.

I can't say it was easy, but by the end of this time I was no longer afraid of being alone. I no longer needed to have someone else in my life in order to feel worthy. I no longer needed—or wanted—to play games and tell lies in order to sleep with a woman. Far from being a frustrating time of neediness, this period of self-restraint was a catalyst for deeper self-understanding. No longer were my days spent fretting over where my next shag was going to come from.

This gave me the strength to resist the most powerful tool women hold over men: sex. It allowed me to see how I had been strung along by my balls in many of my past relationships. So often I had given in to demands just to keep the peace instead of standing strong and making decisions for myself. So often I had been afraid to take the lead and make simple decisions such as what to have for dinner or which restaurant to go to without checking with my partner first to seek her approval. Looking back, I think this probably caused more drama because whoever I was with at the time *wanted* me to take the lead, to show her I was in fact worthy of her attention and desire. In fact, I think she was craving it. She wanted a strong man who would stand up for himself (and her) when it was called for . . . even, ironically, when she was the one being stood up against!

Most men today are confused about the role they are expected to play, both in their relationships and in the wider world. This confusion has arisen over the past generation or so, and it has been a massive blow to our sense of manhood. Women feel the effects too: they know something is missing in their men. To use a military parlance . . . we are off mission.

What is a real man anyway? Is it the guy who's dominant over other men? Or is it the strong guy in touch with his feelings, able to relate to the men and women around him? Is your worth as a man your ability to score another notch on the bedpost in a crazy quest to have sex with as many women as possible? Or is it about finding a great woman to share your life with—someone who can be your lover, best friend, the mother of your kids, someone who'll be there for you no matter what, and you for her?

No one talks about this stuff, but we need to, because when we don't answer these questions we don't mature, and what's the use of that? We're no real use to our mates, our partners or our kids. You only need to observe the mentality of some blokes on a night out, behaving like a pride of lions stalking the Serengeti for their prey, competing for the position of alpha male. It's like watching a scene from a nature show on the Discovery Channel. Some lions will fight viciously against others in their pride as a show of strength that entitles them to mate with any lioness within the group, but we have, supposedly, evolved past the status of common animals—so why do we persist with this idea of what a bloke is?

The problem is that we see things in black and white terms. Do we stick with the traditional model of masculinity, which says men are tough and uncompromising, or do we adopt the new-age idea of the softly spoken and emotionally aware male? I think we are asking the wrong questions here, because true manhood is both of these things and everything in between.

I once witnessed something that will forever stand out in my memory as an example of real manhood—perhaps the most perfect symbol of manhood I could imagine, but from a very unlikely source. It was August 1994 and I had recently begun my training course to become a police dog handler. It was a bitterly cold morning, out in the countryside near the southern highlands town of Goulburn, New South Wales. With a heavy frost covering the vast expanse of the dog training compound in a blanket of white, I was out for a morning walk with my newly acquired canine partner, a young Rottweiler named Dax. We were walking near some low shrubs to allow Dax to relieve himself after a night in the kennels, when his head turned sharply, indicating that something had caught his very acute sense of smell. He ran to the bush and stuck his big head under the foliage. I spoke to him as you would to a small child.

'What have you got there, boy?' I asked.

As his massive head turned and he happily trotted back toward me I noticed he had something in his mouth, clenched delicately between his canines, as if he was carrying an egg. He ever so gently placed it at my feet, giving it an affectionate lick as he did so. It was a baby rabbit.

'Look what I've got for you, Dad,' I could almost hear him say.

What the . . .?

Here was a dog trained to inflict all kinds of damage, an aggressive monster who would in time make even the bravest of men cringe with fear—gently caring for a vulnerable creature like a doting father. It was almost as if he knew the baby rabbit might have died in the frost if he hadn't taken care of it. He seemed to know that he had the power to crush the rabbit's skull—but also that he did not have to.

He chose compassion.

Although I was amazed at what I had seen, I more or less forgot about this incident. It was only years later, when

I started to question what it means to be a man, that the memory came back to me. I realised Dax was the epitome of what I have come to call 'gentle strength'—a way of being that goes against the traditional ideal of manhood, and yet has provided a mental framework that has helped me to overcome anxiety and self-induced suffering.

Once I'd grasped the concept of gentle strength, I understood that my old ideas about manhood were no longer relevant. They were a false map with which I could no longer navigate through life and had outlived their usefulness by about three decades. I needed to throw them away, to be prepared to let my soul fly where it would. Once I'd made the decision to take a new course it felt good. I knew I'd find my way to a better place. Insha Allah, as God wills it . . .

25

Calm and Ease

The seed the Professor had planted had sprouted and blossomed. I was now looking to do more and more things that I would have previously considered uncool. Yes, I had gone on the Sound of Music tour after leaving Iraq and copped insults about it when I got home from many of those who I once called 'mates' but, not really caring about their opinion, I decided to take things to a different level.

In May 2009, more than two and a half years after I'd returned home from Iraq, I was chatting to a friend at a barbecue, telling her about my journey away from the world of special operations and violence toward a more peaceful existence.

'Have you ever tried meditation?' she asked me.

'No.'

'You might like it,' she said.

Even though I was becoming more open to new ideas I'd always thought meditation was a bit out there for my liking.

'There's a place that runs a course up at Blackheath in the Blue Mountains.'

'What's it called?'

'Vipassana. It's a ten-day introduction to meditation.'

'That sounds pretty full-on.'

'It's a challenge.'

'How so?'

'You can't talk for the first nine days and you meditate pretty much all day.'

'Holy shit.'

'But the benefits are amazing. I think you'd be able to handle it.'

'That sounds cool. How much does it cost?'

'It's free. You just make a donation at the end of the course—whatever amount you think is suitable for what you got out of it.'

'Fantastic!'

The next day I applied online for a course coming up in two weeks' time. There was no need to stop and consider anything because it felt right. It was just another stepping stone on a path that takes a lifetime to travel. When I arrived at the meditation centre in its calm, bush setting, I immediately felt a sense of serenity. The stillness was in part the result of 'noble silence': the practice of non-communication that was observed for the first nine days of the ten-day course. In other words: no speaking, no gestures and no physical contact with anybody else on the course.

The routine for the duration of the course was simple. Up at four for two hours' meditation, breakfast, meditation, lunch, meditation, dinner, meditation, then bed, with nothing but the odd contemplative wander on the bushwalking trails within the complex in the middle. No television, books, magazines or anything else that would disturb the goal of clearing the mind. A major focus of the course was to learn the Vipassana technique, a meditation practice that originated in India around 500 BCE. Centred on a breathing technique that allows the mind to clear the clutter built up as part of our daily lives, it encourages openness to new experiences by getting rid of the rubbish we don't need.

For the first few days I struggled with everything: the sitting position (up to twelve hours a day), the early morning rise and the strictly vegetarian diet. Of the one hundred or so participants on the course the ratio of women to men was about three to one with the average age of the women being much younger. This seemed to be proof not only that blokes are resistant to doing things that aren't seen as manly, but also that they see the error of their ways much later in life, too—like I was. Even though I had come so far in the past couple of years as far as personal growth was concerned, sitting in a quiet room with a hundred other people was a real challenge. I wrestled with what I came to understand were very common physical and emotional pains associated with meditation.

On day five, the process of clearing the rubbish of my subconscious began to yield worrying results as fears about the future, the past and myriad other concerns came to the surface.

'Is this normal?' I asked the teacher, the only person with whom we were permitted to speak.

'Yes. When you start to get rid of the stuff you don't need, any fears that have been lurking below the surface will come up.'

Suddenly all my doubts and fears were being released, after all the years I'd spent forcing them down: fears about finances, about finding love, but most importantly, fears about how others would respect me as a man now that I no longer carried a gun and demanded authority.

'Just observe what is coming to the surface and let it go,' the teacher said.

Easy for him to say, I thought, but I heeded his advice anyway. Having taken the first steps some time ago in my quest for a new way of looking at life, I knew that there were going to be some ups and downs. It seemed to be a normal part of the process—a cosmic dance of two steps forward one step back. Life was not always easy, I now knew, and something as simple as 'accepting what is' was going to take time—but I had plenty of that.

The day after my conversation with the teacher I was sitting in the meditation room, acutely aware I'd drifted into an almost hypnotic state as I practiced the art of letting go of any thoughts and feelings that came up. Like the sensation of an elevator suddenly stopping, I felt myself jolt downwards, almost falling as I reached a level of calmness I'd never experienced. Even though my eyes were closed and I was sitting perfectly still with my head to the front I could see the entire room around me. I looked right around the room, my head perfectly still all the while, amazed at this experience, when two white fully formed beings, one female and one male, with human-looking bodies, appeared in front of me carrying a white bucket. They held the bucket forward and gestured for me to take what was inside. I was filled with a feeling of serenity that seemed to dispel any thought of fear and although I sensed they wanted me to accept their offering I very nonchalantly said (in my mind), 'I'm right, thanks.'

They just shrugged their shoulders and walked along the line to the next person and that was it. I don't know if they were ghosts, or what they might have been. I can't explain it, and I'm not even going to try, but the experience was as real as anything else I can remember. Throughout the rest of the course I longed to feel that same high, to see the white beings again, to find out more about them and discover what they had been offering me, but it was all to no avail. Like everything else, I had to let the experience go without craving it.

After remaining silent for nine days, a task that was, in the end, quite easy, I shared this experience with some other participants, and they in turn told me about their own experiences during the course. Of particular note was Geoff, a fifty-odd-year-old guy from Sydney who had come to the course as a means of negotiating a crossroad in his life that was causing him and his family a great deal of distress. During dinner conversation on the last night I picked up that he was experiencing many of the things I had a few years earlier, albeit in a different way.

A successful real estate developer who had built a large investment portfolio and had all the trappings of wealth such as cars, houses and overseas holidays, Geoff spoke of the pain that he was feeling as a result of his inner turmoil. I knew that pain. It was the same pain I had felt when I made the decision to leave my old self behind and I could see that he was going through the same thing.

'I don't want to do it anymore,' Geoff said between spoonfuls of lentil pie.

'Why not?' I asked.

'It just doesn't feel right. I want to do something that I enjoy, not something that makes money.'

'So why don't you?'

'I don't think my wife will let me. She's used to having everything she wants.'

Status symbols such as money, cars and investments are called 'trappings' for good reason. Once in our possession they literally trap us into believing they have some sort of value when in fact they are merely things that come and go over time.

Actually, when you think about . . . so are we. Our physical existence on this planet is only temporary. We are born with nothing and we will die with nothing, so anything in between is and can only ever be temporary.

I wanted Geoff to consider this, so I asked him,

'How does that make you feel?'

'Mate, I feel like I'm trapped. I want to explore stuff and be myself—but if I do that I might lose my family.'

'Do you think your wife will leave you because you want to change?'

'I don't know, maybe.'

'I spoke to an old guy once who told me that if we're not living within our integrity then we cannot be happy.'

'What did he mean by "integrity"?'

It was a moment of déjà vu. I had asked the Professor the very same question those three short years before.

'If we're doing something that's not in line with who we are, then we can't be happy because we're not whole.'

'Oh, okay. I get it. Has it worked for you?'

I spent the next few minutes telling Geoff about the many discoveries I'd made since meeting the Professor. I told him about the difficulties and the rewards associated with the transformation I was making. Most of all I told him how I had felt a great weight lifting off my shoulders when I began striving for a life of greater integrity.

'Have you told your wife about how you feel?' I asked him.

'I brought it up once as a joke and she nearly freaked. I'm a bit reluctant to mention it again because she'll just get the shits.'

'Okay. So when do *you* get what *you* want?'

'What do you mean?'

'Well, how long are you just going to do what everybody else wants you to do?'

'I've never thought of it like that, but isn't that selfish?'

'Mate, if we're always trying to please others because we think we might be rude or selfish or whatever, then when do we really get to experience the things that *we* want?'

I could see Geoff's mind ticking over, just like mine had when I spoke to the Professor.

'And when you think about it, not wanting to offend or to tell someone what you think isn't about not hurting their feelings or protecting them. It's about us not wanting them to think we are rude or offensive.'

Geoff's inability to say what he wanted was only causing frustration. This would continue to build until he could find it within himself to bring more integrity and honesty to his relationship.

'Thank you,' he said as we parted after dinner.

I knew Geoff would be facing a number of challenges and no doubt the biggest would be dealing with the changing dynamic of his family relationship. It would be a time of tough decisions and more than a few tears—but that would be his journey to take. In the meantime, I was continuing on my own journey. Driving away from the course I felt elated, as if another layer of my disguise had been removed.

Continuing to meditate regularly over the next few weeks I noticed I was beginning to apply the practice of meditation in everyday circumstances without needing to sit down in a quiet setting, most noticeably while playing golf. As I walked along the fairways I could hear birds chirping in the distance. I could feel the sensation of the grass beneath my feet and even hear the creak of my knees as I walked. When I reached my ball I was not concerned with how I'd look if I didn't hit it well . . . it didn't matter. I was becoming mindful of all that was around me and was increasingly able to catch myself in the act of what many eastern philosophies call 'suffering'—clinging onto thoughts that bring unhappiness or feeling sadness at the loss of material possessions. The Professor might have said that I was starting, slowly but surely, to be guided by my soul rather than driven by my ego. Many of my former concerns began to dissipate and were replaced by a feeling of calm and ease. Calm and ease when I stood over a golf ball. Calm and ease when I walked down the street. Calm and ease when I talked with my children. Calm and ease when confronted with difficult situations. Calm and ease when I communicated with other men.

I no longer felt the need to defend anything.

I no longer felt the need to seek anyone's approval.

I no longer felt the need to react blindly without knowing why.

I no longer felt the need to compete for the position of alpha male.

But as I said, challenges would always be forthcoming.

26

Don't Mistake Kindness for Weakness

A few months after Vipassana, the feeling of inner peace was tested to its limits. Sitting in a hotel in the Rocks district of Sydney with a group of friends one evening, I noticed a guy staring at me from across the room. It felt a lot like the atmosphere before the bar room brawl in Cessnock.

Oh, c'mon dude, I don't do this shit anymore, I thought, realising that he must be picking up on remnants of the facade that had served me for so long. I mean, physically I was the same person. I still exercised (though not to the same intensity), so it was also possible he saw me as a threat to his territory and he was trying to protect it. Whatever he was picking up on he wasn't happy. A pretty fit-looking but about average-sized bloke, he was surrounded by several mates who appeared to hang off his coat-tails. He was definitely the leader of this bunch.

Not wanting to let any shenanigans spoil what had been a pleasant night, I ignored what was going on. Although I wanted to avoid confrontation at just about any cost, I turned my chair so that I would at least see him coming in my peripheral vision if that's what he chose to do.

Soon after I saw him walk slowly across the room toward our group with a couple of his entourage in close formation behind. Walking like he was carrying two watermelons under his armpits with his chest puffed out like a pigeon he stopped about five metres away and pretended to talk to his mates, all the time looking in my direction.

I didn't bother to return his stare. I was done playing the macho bullshit dominance game.

It was then that Lisa, a girl within our group, noticed what was going on.

'Shane, that guy keeps looking at you,' she said, motioning toward the guy with her eyes.

It was funny to hear my real name again. I hadn't been called Horse since I'd lost contact with many of my old workmates.

'Yeah, I know. He's been looking at me for about ten minutes.'

'What are you going to do?' she asked.

'Absolutely nothing.'

I didn't need to prove anything to anyone.

'He's coming over,' Lisa said, a hint of panic in her voice.

I turned around and looked directly at the guy and smiled. Not the type of smile that would suggest I was a smart-arse or that I knew something he didn't; it was a genuine smile of friendship. He looked a little confused.

Wasn't I supposed to challenge his position?

Didn't I want to look good in front of the girls?

Whatever he was thinking, he walked off, his hangers close behind him.

'What happened there?' Lisa asked.

'Instead of meeting him with fear or aggression, I met him with a smile and a bit of compassion.'

'Well it worked!'

'Of course . . . it's an old Jedi mind trick.'

We both laughed as I thought to myself how the Professor and a few other teachers along the way had gotten me to this moment of clarity. When I say 'a few other teachers', I also mean the less obvious ones like ex-partners, old colleagues and those with whom I may have had conflict in the past. Each one has caused me to examine my own behaviour, helping me to see clearly what life would be like if I stopped playing the alpha male game. The game is, and can only ever be, fleeting. There is always someone around the corner who is tougher, faster, bigger or younger—a fact reflected in nature. Look at the life of a dominant silverback gorilla, for example, at the top of his social hierarchy. We might think this would be a great position to hold, always in control, the master of our domain, with the exclusive right to 'service' any of the females in the group, but in fact the dominant male is constantly challenged by other males. His reign at the top is a stressful time of never-ending vigilance as he tries to predict where his next challenge is going to come from.

And so it is with humans.

Chasing the top position is not only stressful, it also prohibits us from being who we really are. Does it really matter if you back down from a fight when somebody is challenging you? Is it really a mark of manhood to dominate friends, spouses or work colleagues to the point that these relationships fail? Do we really want to be in constant conflict with our supervisors or bosses? Does it really matter if we are not seen to be the king of the hill? Surely not. I would like to think our species has evolved beyond these primal survival games.

So where does it begin to go wrong for guys? I guess it begins in childhood, but where exactly? I had a fairly normal childhood. Long summer days spent riding my bike along country roads with friends or playing 'wars' in the bush with a stick as a machine gun. In my teens it was rollerskating around the local school with a few mates and some girls we fancied, trying to find an excuse to encourage one of them behind the weather shed to steal a quick kiss.

Looking back everything seemed as it should be—but at some point in my development, I put on a mask.

Was it a perceived lack of attention from my parents while I was growing up? Was it a feeling of abandonment when I really needed to be loved? Was it the 'children should be seen but not heard' or the 'do as I say, not as I do' mentality? I honestly don't know. I think we have a tendency as children to put our parents on a pedestal that is unrealistic and potentially damaging to us. I remember thinking my dad was the smartest, strongest man alive;

I was in awe of his ability to catch me even when I was running as fast as my six-year-old legs would go. I revered him without ever knowing why. As I grew older, still believing that parents are infallible, I never subjected this assumption to any scrutiny—but at an unconscious level I think I knew my father was not as perfect as I had imagined. He was just doing the best he could with the mask he himself had created to cope with his own childhood.

I have distinct memories, from a very young age, of visiting my grandparents with my family. The womenfolk were left in the kitchen to make the tea while the men— my grandfather, father and me—went out to the shed and talked about men's stuff. A woman's presence would only be tolerated if she was delivering a cuppa—and she wasn't welcome to stick around afterward. Even as a young boy my grandfather's behaviour struck me as a bit odd. I never really liked him. Even to a young boy he always seemed cranky and opinionated and when I found out years later he had a violent, explosive temper the pieces of the jigsaw puzzle finally fell into place. I realised that under my grandfather's watchful eye my father had never been able to express himself freely and openly for fear of punishment, causing him to develop his own ways of protecting himself from emotional and/or physical harm. Sadly, I suspect my grandfather grew up in a similar environment.

Almost like a game of Chinese whispers, where the original message is garbled as it is passed on, and eventually distorted beyond recognition, each generation was passing on a way of parenting that, left unchecked, would become more and more dysfunctional. It's easy to play the victim and start pointing the finger, trying to establish why things are the way they are, but it's a pointless exercise that just breeds more resentment and anger. Refusing to adopt this approach has allowed me to feel nothing but compassion for both men and recognise that no one is to blame.

So many adult men are still fighting against the demons of their childhood. They are trapped by their upbringing, unable to fully express themselves, always wanting to maintain the illusion of being in control at all times. I am filled with a deep sadness when I look at how many guys from generations past have gone through life without ever being able to be real, pretending to be strong, silent types or emotional stalwarts instead of being authentic. They may have seen their friends or family killed during any number of bitter wars, or experienced financial hardship during the Great Depression, but did they ever really feel comfortable expressing their grief? Personal experience tells me they did not; many, like my grandfather, took their real feelings of unexpressed anger, grief, sadness or even happiness to the grave.

When you think about it, how many blokes are willing to admit they're not able to cope with a situation or that they don't have the skills to do something they've been asked to do? How many blokes refuse to back down from conflict so as to save face? I know I found it hard to do these things. It undermined my ability to maintain a loving marriage. It stifled my ability to develop close and valued friendships. It caused conflict when it could have been avoided. Unfortunately, this constant struggle for control is played out on the world stage every day—and, as the Professor said, this will only improve when men find peace within themselves.

As an individual, the only thing I can do now is become more aware of my own behaviour, to allow my children to develop and grow without taking on my baggage. It is not something I can simply tell them—it is something I have to become. By being honest in everything I do and say. Showing them open and genuine affection so they feel supported, or demonstrating discipline and consistency in my decision-making. Establishing trust in their word in the absence of hard facts or even showing vulnerability in the face of new challenges. As a parent, I do not demand respect or trust, but try to earn it, and I am certainly not seeking to be placed on a pedestal. I am, and always will be, a work in progress.

Gaining a deeper understanding of how childhood experiences had shaped my life and then moving beyond them to do things in a different way has been instrumental in awakening the true warrior within me—a very different creature to the old Horse, the tough guy who carried a gun.

27

Awaken the Warrior

Along with what we see, hear and learn from our parents and family, the wider environment in which we grow up undoubtedly plays an integral role in shaping our view of manhood, albeit a confusing one. On the one hand we are expected to be this tough hero who doesn't show his emotions, but on the other hand we are supposed to be sensitive new-age guys. Our mates expect us to act one way around them, and then our partners and kids expect something completely different. So which one is right? Who do we please?

Adding to this confusion is our habit of making role models out of ordinary people we see on TV, like sports stars, politicians, celebrities and religious leaders. Men want to measure up to these 'heroes', but we are doomed to fail because the idea of manhood we get from TV is an illusion. We are modelling ourselves on made-up characters. Not only are these people human, but in some cases they are seriously flawed. Whether they are cheating on their wives, girlfriends or partners, lying to get ahead in business, treading on others in a quest for glory, or taking advantage of positions of authority in order to dominate others, one thing is for sure—they are not deserving of our attention, let alone our admiration. They are not really men—they are boys using their influence or power to cover up self-esteem issues they have never addressed.

A man's role used to be clear. It was precise and defined: breadwinner, protector, procreator and patriarch. We are still expected to be these things to some degree, but our role in the world has become increasingly blurred. We put pressure on ourselves trying to live up to the expectations of society, but it's hard now to define exactly what these expectations are—what we are supposed to be. So what happens when we fall short? Ask any guy whose 'perfect' family is torn apart by divorce, or who thought his job would last forever, or who feels he is not where he is supposed to be financially by a certain age, and the answer will be simple. It causes a crisis, just as it had in me. Unfortunately there are a disturbing number of guys who reach this crisis point and see no way out of the darkness that inevitably descends when it happens, choosing to commit suicide as a means of dealing with the pain. In Australia, men account for nearly eighty per cent of all suicides, and the majority of those are aged from their late thirties to early forties.

Imagine if these guys had been able to talk honestly and openly with a mate to sort out some problems.

Imagine if they had been able to cry and express their grief without fear of being ridiculed or seen as weak. This is a dire problem that needs to be addressed so future generations of men can learn to do things in a different and hopefully healthier way. I know from experience that this change won't be easy, but I believe the mental anguish I experienced as I moved away from my old identity was a natural part of the process. The fear, anxiety and doubt I went through caused me to reflect on my behaviours and beliefs and then, eventually, to make a choice. I chose to stop behaving like a boy and start being a man; to stop pretending I was something I wasn't. I consciously chose to develop the type of integrity the Professor had spoken so highly of by tapping into the warrior within us all.

So what does a true warrior really look like? What does it really mean to be courageous? Is it really an important part of being a man? In modern times words like hero, courage and warrior are often used as an easy way of expressing admiration for actions on the battlefield or in the sporting arena, but these are mostly throwaway lines that do not do these descriptions justice.

The measure of a true warrior is not about how many fights we have had, or how many dangerous operations or battles we have been in, or how many notches we can get on the bedpost. True 'warriorhood' is about unlocking the door to mature masculinity by becoming a strong, gentle, compassionate man and having the integrity to stay strong and balanced in the face of challenges. To stay strong when your mates try to shame you into having another drink when you know you've had enough. To stay strong when you feel under pressure to do something you don't want to because you want to fit in. To stay strong when your mates realise the new 'you' is different to what they are used to. Daring to go against, or at least seriously question, how we have been brought up and conditioned over the years and look for new ways of living that are better for our health, relationships and happiness. This is the path of a true warrior. By working to develop mature masculine qualities, we can build a bridge between how we are now and what we would like to become.

I'd like to look specifically at three of these mature human qualities: awareness, courage and discipline. I have chosen these three because they encompass so many others and each of them is crucial to achieving a fully adult form of masculinity.

Before my conversation with the Professor, I was almost completely unaware of what I was doing, how my upbringing had shaped me and how I was strung along by my ego. Since that fateful day, I have learned to be conscious of what goes on around me and how it affects my life. If I find that somebody has a different opinion, I no longer reject it as wrong; I can accept their viewpoint. If I am stuck in bad traffic or another driver does something to make me angry, I understand what is driving the emotion and try not let it get the better of me. This growing awareness is helping me to catch myself in the act of suffering. My eyes are now open and life has become more peaceful and enjoyable because of it.

I understand now that all guys have a feminine part of their psyche that needs as much attention as the masculine aspect if we are to live in integrity as balanced, strong, compassionate men. If we refuse to acknowledge its existence we are denying a part of ourselves that enables good, close, loving relationships to form. I think many men feel ambivalent toward their partner because they don't have enough understanding of themselves and their own feminine side to consider a better way of approaching things. Preferring to adopt the 'can't live with them, can't live without them' mantra, some guys go through relationship after relationship never learning anything from the experience. Never learning that by acknowledging their own feminine side they will allow themselves to be more open, compassionate and forgiving instead of fearing what they do not understand. I'm convinced that this fear of the unknown lurks behind damaging attitudes like homophobia; some guys are so uncomfortable with the female part of themselves that they will call others 'faggots' and 'poofters' to distance themselves from it. The same goes for guys who seem to hate women, to the point of inflicting extreme violence and abuse on them. Like it or not, the path to integrity requires the building of a bridge between these two parts of our soul.

I now have a better understanding of action and consequence, knowing that a great deal of what I get in life is a result of the actions I have taken or the beliefs I hold. If I am rude or arrogant I can expect the same in return. If I am not open to changes happening around me I can expect to become irritated and unsure. If I do not respect the relationship I am in and take time to nurture it, it will fail.

Epictetus, a Greek philosopher born in the first century AD, said that 'people are not disturbed by things, but the view they take of them'. What I think he was saying is that the more rigidly we stick to a viewpoint, position, belief or opinion, the greater the crisis when that is proven to be false or misleading. When I spoke to the Professor he talked about how clinging strongly to our beliefs—so strongly that we are willing to fight and/or die for them— is what causes most conflict in the world. By remaining open, by being willing to question the beliefs we hold, we can achieve a calm and ease that would otherwise be impossible. It is okay to accept opposing points of view— both may be valid. It is okay for others to do things differently to us. It is okay to live in a paradoxical world with nothing really set in stone.

The more I have learned and researched and read and listened over the past few years, the less I know for sure. Our existence is shaped by opinions, beliefs and custom instead of hard facts. Strangely, accepting this contradiction—*the more I learn, the less I know*—has made life easier and much less complicated. Luckily there are no final exams or pass/fail marks to determine if we have been successful. The only gauge of progress in this endeavour is our ability to rethink our actions when needed without hanging on too tightly to what may be outdated beliefs.

Living in awareness is about constantly observing ego. It is about asking questions. Some questions you need to ask yourself on the spot: 'Do I really want another beer?' Others are ongoing: 'What do I really want from this relationship?' or perhaps 'Is this job right for me?' If we constantly ask these questions, we can catch ourselves in the act of suffering. It creates space between our thoughts and actions and helps us get a good hold of the leash to get the dog back under control.

After awareness comes courage. I am always inspired by stories of people who have sought to think for themselves, being courageous enough to follow their own moral code instead of going with the crowd, even when it might have been dangerous to do so. Our modern idea of courage has been distorted by Hollywood and the media, and has only served to make men feel more inadequate. True courage is something we all have in us. Quite simply, courage means questioning and perhaps even rejecting all the training and conditioning that were part of your upbringing, even if it scares you to death. If you resist the pressure from your mates to do something you don't want to, that is courage. If you express emotion openly when it is appropriate, that is courage. If you choose to take a more proactive approach to your relationship, that is courage. If you choose to look at the world as one of possibilities instead of competition, that is courage. As the Professor said, 'Over time you will learn to walk the fine line between a hero and a coward. That is true courage.'

The infamous My Lai massacre that took place during the Vietnam War was a tragic incident, but it prompted an act of bravery that I find inspirational, one that epitomises the type of courage I have been referring to. On 16 March 1968 a company of US soldiers undertook an operation to clear the village of My Lai of Vietcong soldiers and sympathisers. Eyewitness accounts from both sides describe what happened next as something that would not be out of place in a horror movie. In a frenzy lasting several hours approximately five hundred women and children from the village were rounded up, beaten and then slaughtered like cattle by the US soldiers using rifles, bayonets and grenades.

As the bodies began to pile up a US helicopter pilot who was flying overhead, Warrant Officer Hugh Thompson, observing the slaughter, saw a group of unarmed women and children cowering in a ditch near the village with a platoon of US soldiers moving toward them. Thompson landed his helicopter between the advancing soldiers and the civilians, instructing the machine gunner on the side of the chopper to point his weapon at the advancing soldiers and 'shoot if necessary' to protect the women and children, saving several lives in the process. Thompson had listened to his own sense of moral right and wrong and risked his life by going against his military training. I would suggest that he possessed a well-developed inner feminine energy that allowed him to show compassion for fellow human beings whereas the advancing soldiers had been conditioned to repress theirs. Thompson's actions, along with those of his crew, are a perfect example of the courage that comes from wholeness—from integrity.

Finally, after awareness and courage, comes discipline. Once a warrior has the awareness to recognise and analyse his own thoughts, feelings and behavioural patterns, and the courage to follow his own moral code (even when he risks being ridiculed by others), discipline is required to maintain the momentum. Not the type of discipline imposed by military or police organisations, but the kind that will allow personal growth to occur well into the future. Only with discipline can we achieve mature masculinity, and overcome the difficulties that may occur along the way. Discipline helps us to maintain inner balance so we do not place too much emphasis on the peripheral things in life such as the pursuit of material possessions or superficial relationships. Discipline helps us to set an example for others to follow because when we are disciplined we are not easily affected by the ups and downs of life.

Awareness, courage and discipline have helped me to integrate the different aspects of my personality and make me whole. In stark contrast to the days when I was pulled around blindly by neediness and insecurity, I now feel an inner strength and happiness. I recently got back to doing something I had enjoyed as a teenager and then forgotten about during my twenties and thirties—musical theatre. I could never have admitted to this interest during my time as a tactical operator for fear of the sledging I would have received. When I was approached recently to audition for a singing, dancing and acting role in a local musical theatre production, for a fleeting moment I thought *How is this going to look?* A few years ago I would have rejected the invitation outright, worried about how others might see me, but as I grow and learn my desire to try new things and to meet new people has also grown, and it overruled any doubts I had. Performing on stage with a mix of people from different cultures, backgrounds and viewpoints has been an enlightening and thoroughly enjoyable experience, and good for my soul. It really feels like my life has come full circle. As my true self emerges from beneath the layers of ego, I am moving away from boyhood thinking and taking confident strides toward becoming a real man. The inner warrior is awake now, and ready to face the world.

Epilogue
Lessons Learned

When I first made it known I was committing my thoughts to paper, many of my friends assumed it would be a collection of 'war' stories and tales of near misses and drama associated with my previous vocation. In truth, though my time with the police and in Iraq provides a colourful backdrop, this book is about the liberation of my soul. It is about the freedom that comes from combining traditional masculinity with traits that are typically regarded as feminine, such as compassion, empathy and love—integrating these supposed opposites into one person. I believe this is what it takes to become not just a well-functioning man, but also fully human, just as the Professor suggested. By sharing my story—both the good and bad experiences—I want to help other men follow their own path, but hopefully with fewer obstacles. In essence, this book is not really about me—it is every man's story.

I'd like to finish this book by sharing the most powerful life lessons I have learned along the way.

It's important to grow as a human being, not just as a man

Our ideas about what it means to be a man limit our opportunities for growth, because men in our society have traditionally been discouraged from talking about or acknowledging their feelings—a vital step in understanding ourselves. We are also taught to judge ourselves through the eyes of others, seeing ourselves as they see us. These judgements are superficial, based on external appearances.

Men tend to fight against personal growth, because it means doing things we haven't done before, uncomfortable things that make us feel strange and uneasy, like discussing our emotions, or admitting to our doubts and fears in front of others—things that women are 'allowed' to do that we are not. It's natural to prefer to stick with the status quo—it's familiar, and relatively easy, compared with the complex path that is inner growth—but we have to get past this if we want to embrace our true, full selves and become mature adults.

While taking the first steps is tough, the good news is that it gets much easier. When we open up, expressing not just our fears and doubts but also our hopes and our passion, life is more meaningful and far more rewarding—and when we listen to our inner selves, consciously committing ourselves to growth, the beliefs and opinions of others start to seem less important.

Feelings of unworthiness are a like a cancer of the soul

Feeling unworthy is one of the main reasons we drift so far from our true selves and is a major cause of suffering among humans. To counteract these feelings we make up stories to make ourselves look better or tell lies to cover up insecurities. It can even make us unconsciously sabotage our relationships because we do not feel worthy of happiness. Realising that everyone is worthy of love, respect and happiness is the only cure for this insidious disease.

The observing, understanding and mastering of ego is vital to quell the inner voices of conflict

Observing, understanding and mastering my ego will be a lifetime challenge. I still find it useful to think of my ego as dog, a comparison that first occurred to me more than six years ago now, during my conversation with the Professor. An untamed ego drags its owner around the streets instead of walking calmly next to them as a companion—and, as with dogs, the secret is loving discipline.

When I find myself facing conflict, whether it's at work or in my private life, I try to stop for a second and identify the underlying emotions I'm feeling and where they are coming from. Perhaps I'm feeling irritation, or anger, or hurt. Then I ask myself some fundamental questions, such as 'What is causing this feeling?' or 'What beliefs or assumptions am I bringing to this situation, and how have they been challenged?' I use this simple process to determine whether my ego is taking control or whether I am making choices based on good judgement. Taking a few seconds out to determine what's really going on underneath is always worthwhile.

Even the best-trained dogs occasionally misbehave but that's only to be expected. It's okay to acknowledge your lapses into ego-driven behaviour and move on. Knowing and understanding what drives our decisions and actions can only be achieved through regular, long-term observation of our ego and its motivations. It definitely helps to maintain a sense of humour—specifically, the ability to laugh at ourselves or at the human condition, rather than at the expense of others. Humour helps us to accept human nature and the world as they are, to love and respect ourselves and others, and to enjoy ourselves without regret or apology.

Nothing is black and white

When we accept the fact that life is not simple, we are able to transcend its complexities and live simply. Once we have grasped this paradox, our ability to cope with life's challenges is greatly increased.

This paradox takes many forms. Everyone has experienced the paradox of effort: the harder we try, the worse things get, but when we relax and don't try so hard, things fall into place. Then there's the paradox of money: working long hours to provide for your family, only to see these loved ones pushed away by your absence. Control is another of life's paradoxes: it is only when you give up the idea of achieving total control that you gain maximum control. Finally, and perhaps most importantly, there's the paradox of insignificance: it's only when we embrace our insignificance in this vast world that we can make a significant difference.

Everyone has something to offer

As we cast off the shackles of tribalism and begin to see the world as one community we are better able to go beyond our own cultural conditioning, learning from anyone, regardless of race, religion, class or gender; just as I did in Iraq. Armed with humility and a friendly disposition, we can make new friends who will teach us new ways of thinking, feeling and being. Exposure to different ways of life can help us identify our own shortfalls and weaknesses, giving us the opportunity to make changes in our lives for the better.

Every day, in my capacity as an educator, I learn that people of all ages, genders and cultures have vast knowledge and experience to share, and accepting this fact is essential for my growth as a human being.

I am a work in progress

Enough said.